NAVAL CHRONICLE

1799–1818

Index to Births, Marriages and Deaths

compiled by Norman Hurst

Published Privately – 1989

Naval Chronicle 1799 – 1818
Index to Births, Marriages and Deaths

Published privately by
Norman Hurst
25, Byron Avenue
Coulsdon
Surrey CR3 2JS

ISBN
1 872497 00 4 (paperback)
1 872497 01 2 (loose leaf)

Computer typeset by
Groundwork, Grange-over-Sands, Cumbria
from original text prepared by the author on
an Amstrad PCW9512 word processor

Printed by
Stramongate Press, Kendal, Cumbria

Contents

About this book

The Naval Chronicle was issued in monthly parts from the beginning of 1799 until the end of 1818 when publication ceased. Complete sets are now rare and expensive.

The modest volume here presented seeks to provide a short cut for naval and family historians by presenting in alpha/chronological order the names to be found in the forty volumes of that work under the headings of Births, Marriages and Obituaries (including deaths recorded in Letters of Service extracted from the London Gazette) and biographical memoirs. The Sailor's Home Journal (afterwards The Naval Chronicle) 1853-1863 is not covered.

Experience has shown that background can be obtained about officers whose careers were cut short in the service of their country and who do not feature, therefore, in the standard naval biographies published from 1820 onwards. Unfortunately there is no standard format for the reports so that some are tantalisingly brief whereas others go into interesting detail. Similarly precise dates are not always given, 'lately' is a popular description,as are 'ult.' and 'inst.',for this reason I have prefaced this work with a table showing the months covered by each volume in an effort to help users identify the particular period in time in which they may be interested.

Within the alphabetical listing, names have been sorted in the chronological order in which they appear in the Chronicle first by volume then by page. Although there are cases where particular names recur the absence of uniformity in reporting events make it impossible to present the information in an ideal format. The method adopted provides a practical compromise.

In cases where initials or christian names are not recorded or where two names are identical I have amplified the entry, wherever possible, with additional information. The absence or otherwise of such notes is no indication of the extent of the entry in the Naval Chronicle.

Whilst every care has been taken in the preparation and production of this index it is inevitable that with some twenty thousand pages of text to scan errors may have occurred. Caxton recognised the problem in presenting his work to the public when he wrote "Pardone me where I have erryd or made fawte, whyche yf ony be is of ygnoraunce and ageyn my wylle". My efforts will be amply rewarded, however, by the thought that some users will be fortunate enough to discover details about an ancestor that might otherwise have gone unnoticed.

Abbreviations

AB . . . . Able Seaman
Adm . . . Admiral
Adm'y . . . Admiralty
Battn . . . Battalion
Capt . . . . Captain
Ch . . . . . Church
Col . . . . Colonel
Comm . . . Commodore
Commiss . Commissioner
Corp . . . . Corporal
dau . . . . daughter
Dr . . . . . Doctor
Drag . . . Dragoon
FRS . . . . Fellow of the Royal Society
Gds . . . . Guards
Gen . . . . General
HEIC . . . Honourable East India Company
Hon . . . . Honourable
IoW . . . . Isle of Wight
Lt . . . . . Lieutenant
m . . . . . married
MD . . . . Doctor of Medicine
Mid . . . . Midshipman
MP . . . . Member of Parliament
p.o.w. . . . prisoner of war
Pte . . . . Private
QM . . . . Quartermaster
RA . . . . Royal Artillery
R Adm . . Rear Admiral
RE . . . . Royal Engineers
Regmt . . . Regiment
Rev . . . . Reverend
RM . . . . Royal Marines
RMA . . . Royal Marine Artillery
RN . . . . Royal Navy
Sgn . . . . Surgeon
Sgt . . . . Sergeant
V Adm . . Vice Admiral
Vis . . . . Viscount

Naval Chronicle
1799-1818

Jan-June Volume No		Year	July-Dec Volume No	
1		1799		2
3	(Jan-July)	1800	(July-Jan)	4
5	(Jan-July)	1801		6
7	(Jan-July)	1802		8
9	(Jan-July)	1803		10
11	(Jan-July)	1804		12
13		1805		14
15		1806		16
17		1807		18
19		1808		20
21		1809		22
23		1810		24
25		1811		26
27		1812		28
29		1813		30
31		1814		32
33		1815		34
35		1816		36
37		1817		38
39		1818		40

BIRTHS

Arnold	Lt RN	28.438	a daughter
Austen C	Capt RN	28.512	a son
Austin	Capt RN	25.439	a son
Austin	Capt RN	31.87	a daughter
Ayscough	Capt RN	29.263	a daughter
Bailey	Lt RN	28.87	a daughter
Bakely William		18.437	twin boys
Baker J	Capt RN	13.85	a son
Balfour	Capt RN	31.175	at Portsea, a son
Ballard	Capt RN	8.352	a daughter
Ballard S	Capt RN	11.421	a daughter
Ballard S J	Capt RN	15.176	a son
Ballard S	Capt RN	18.519	a son
Ballard S	Capt RN	21.444	a son
Ballard Volant V	Capt RN	28.87	a daughter
Barrow J		13.164	a son
Barrow John		20.79	a son
Barrow John		23.264	a son
Barrow John		26.438	a daughter
Bashford	Capt RN	24.437	a daughter
Bashford	Capt RN	27.437	a son
Bathurst Walter	Capt RN	21.86	a son
Bathurst	Capt RN	26.438	a son
Bayley William		28.262	a son
Bayntun H	R AdmSir	34.176	a daughter
Becher	Capt RN	22.519	a son
Becher Alexander	Capt RN	37.518	a son
Bedford Frederick		19.175	a son
Bedford	Lt	21.176	of Royal Hospital Greenwich, a son
Bedford Charles		22.88	a son
Bedford Frederick	Lt	29.263	a son
Belcher Nathaniel		15.87	a daughter
Bell	Dr	30.87	of Plymouth, stillborn
Bell	Dr	32.262	a son
Bentinck	Capt RN	14.511	a son
Berkeley	Adm	15.351	a son
Bertie	Capt Hon	25.439	a son
Bingham Joseph	Capt RN	22.175	a daughter
Bingham A B	Capt RN	31.262	a son
Birch Jonathan	Capt HEIC	21.175	a son
Bishop Charles		25.439	a son (14th Child)
Blackwood Henry	Capt Hon	19.439	a son
Blackwood	Capt Hon	21.444	a son
Blanchard J	Capt HEIC	26.263	a son
Blatchford Isabella	Lady	32.262	a son
Booth G		26.263	a daughter
Bourcher	Capt RN	9.250	a son
Bourchier	Capt RN	29.263	a daughter
Bourchier	Capt RN	32.175	a son
Boutan	Capt	10.175	twins
Bouverie	Capt RN, Hon	25.262	a daughter
Boyle Courtenay	Capt Hon	21.86	?
Boyle Courtenay	Capt Hon	24.437	a daughter
Boyle Courtenay	Comm Hon	32.87	a son

Name	Rank	Ref	Note
Bradley	Lt RN	28.262	a daughter
Bremer	Lt RN	9.165	a son
Brenton	Capt RN	9.81	a son
Brenton J	Capt RN	17.176	a son
Bridport	Viscount	33.87	a son
Bright H	Capt RM	8.352	a son
Britain	Capt RM	26.178	a daughter
Brittain	Capt RM	29.87	a son
Broke	Capt RN	27.437	a son
Broke Philip P B V	Sir	33.440	a daughter
Bromley Samuel		23.349	a son
Bromley Robert Howe	Sir	32.351	a daughter
Brown William	Capt RN	14.261	a daughter
Brown T	Capt RN	20.423	a daughter
Brown	Capt RN	24.174	at Greenock, a daughter
Brown Thomas	Capt RN	29.263	a son
Buckle	Capt RN	8.352	a son
Buckle	Capt	13.423	a son
Buckle	Capt RN	16.352	a daughter
Buckle	Capt RN	20.423	a son
Buckle M	Capt	23.264	a daughter
Buller James		25.439	a son
Burdett	Capt RN	9.497	a daughter
Burdwood T	Lt	29.87	a son
Burt	Capt RN	28.176	a daughter
Butt	Capt RN	21.86	stillborn
Butt	Capt RN	24.437	a daughter
Butterfield	Capt RN	14.261	a son
Butterfield	Capt RN	19.263	a son
Butterfield	Capt RN	23.519	a daughter
Butterfield W	Capt RN	30.521	a daughter
Butterfield	Capt RN	34.176	a son
Byng George	Capt RN	28.262	a son & daughter
Byron	Capt RN	10.350	a son
Cadogan George	Capt RN, Hon	25.85	a daughter
Cadogan George	Capt RN, Hon	27.174	a son
Campbell James		24.252	a son
Campbell Robert	Capt RN	24.514	a daughter
Campbell James		27.514	a daughter
Carden	Capt RN	32.175	a daughter
Carruthers Walter	of HEIC	20.255	?
Carter Charles	Capt RN	26.514	a son
Cartier C	Capt RN	11.421	a daughter
Caulfield	Capt RN	10.350	a daughter
Caulfield T Gordon	Capt	28.438	a son
Caulfield	Capt RN	30.521	a son
Caulfield Gordon	Capt RN	33.511	a daughter
Chambers Samuel	Capt RN	19.514	a daughter
Champion	Lt RN	9.165	a son
Champion	Lt RN	13.335	a daughter
Cheeseman	Lt RN	18.437	at Portsea, a daughter
Chetham Edward	Capt RN	29.263	a son
Chetham Edward	Capt	32.438	a daughter
Christian	Capt	24.514	a son
Christian	Capt RN	31.438	a son

Christopher H	Capt HEIC	22.519	a son
Clement	Capt RN	30.264	a son
Cochrane L J	Sir	33.87	a daughter
Cockburn	Comm	27.264	a daughter
Cockcraft W		27.264	a son
Cocks	Capt RN	32.87	two daughters
Codrington E	Capt RN	33.87	a daughter
Collier F	Capt RN	27.264	a son
Coombe	Major RM	29.439	a daughter
Cramer	Capt RN	24.514	a daughter
Cumberland W		20.166	a son
Cumberland William	Capt RN	32.351	a son (9th child)
Cunningham	Mr	26.514	at Portsmouth, a son
Curry	Capt RN	13.423	a daughter
Curry	Capt RN	20.493	a son
Dacres	Capt RN	32.511	a son
Dashwood	Capt RN	6.434	a son
Dashwood	Capt RN	13.164	a son
Davidson	Lt RN	31.87	a daughter
Deans	V Adm	14.261	a daughter
Desborough	Col RM	13.245	a daughter
Desborough	Lt Col RM	16.264	a son
Dewsnap Joseph	Lt	22.175	a daughter
Dick John	Capt RN	20.423	a daughter
Dickson D I H		29.87	a daughter
Dickson Arch	Sir	33.440	a son
Digby Henry	Capt RN	31.87	stillborn daughter
Dix	Capt RN	29.511	a son
Dobbie	Capt RN	24.351	a daughter
Douglas W H	Lt RN	28.176	a daughter
Douglas W H	Capt RN	32.438	at Stonehouse, a
		32.511	daughter
Downman	Capt	12.255	a son
Drummond Adam	Capt RN	21.351	a daughter
Drummond Charlotte	Lady	31.511	a son
Drury	Lt RN	11.175	a son
Duckworth J T	Adm Sir	24.174	a daughter
Duff James	Sir	11.87	a son
Dunn	Capt RN	26.438	a son
Dutton W	Lt RN	26.438	a daughter
Elliot W	Capt RN	26.178	a son
Elliot W	Capt	29.511	a daughter
Elmore Robert		15.351	two boys & a girl
Elphinstone	Capt RN	7.364	a daughter
Elphinstone	Capt RN	10.175	a daughter
Evelyn	Lt RN	9.339	three daughters
Eyre	Capt RN	14.511	a son
Farquhar	Capt RN	26.438	a son
Farquhar Arthur	Capt RN	33.87	a son
Fegen R		32.262	a son
Fisher Peter	Capt RN	32.351	a daughter
Fitzgerald	Capt RN	29.351	a son
Flinders	Capt RN	27.514	a daughter
Foote	Capt RN	17.176	a daughter

Fowke George	Capt	**29**.351	a daughter
Franklin J R	Capt HEIC	**20**.335	a son
Franklyn J R	Capt HEIC	**23**.439	a daughter
Gallaway	Capt RN	**30**.521	a son
Gamble William Robt.		**28**.351	a daughter
Gardner W H	Hon	**20**.166	a daughter
Gardner	Adm Lord	**23**.264	a son
Gardner W H	Hon	**24**.85	a daughter
Gardner	R Adm Lord	**25**.85	a daughter
Gardner F F	Capt Hon	**28**.176	a son
Gardner	R Adm Hon	**31**.175	a son
Garrett H	Capt RN	**17**.352	a son
Gifford	Capt RN	**30**.447	a son
Giles Samuel		**28**.438	a son & daughter
Goddard Thomas		**17**.439	a son & daughter
Goddard T		**26**.178	a son
Gold	Major RA	**24**.351	a daughter
Gomm James		**19**.263	a daughter
Goodridge	Lt HEIC	**30**.175	a daughter
Goold	Lady	**16**.264	a son
Gordon J M	Capt RN	**26**.438	a son
Gore J	Capt Sir	**23**.264	a daughter
Gore John	Sir	**25**.352	a daughter
Gore John	Sir	**28**.262	a son
Gosselin T Le	Capt	**25**.513	a daughter
Gosselin	R Adm	**32**.175	a daughter
Graham Charles	Capt	**19**.439	a son
Graham Charles	Capt HEIC	**24**.85	a son
Grant Thomas		**28**.512	a daughter
Grey	Countess	**25**.85	at Howick, a son
Griffiths	Capt RN	**25**.85	a daughter
Halkett	Capt RN	**15**.87	a daughter
Halkett	Capt RN	**23**.519	stillborn
Halkett	Capt RN	**26**.263	a daughter
Hall Edward		**22**.88	a son
Halliday	Capt RN	**28**.352	a daughter
Halloran L B	Lt RM	**27**.174	a son
Halloran	Lt RM	**31**.438	a son
Hamilton Edward	Sir	**20**.79	a son
Hamilton Edward	Capt Sir	**23**.264	a son
Hamilton Ed	Capt RN, Sir	**27**.264	a daughter
Hamond	Capt RN	**26**.350	a son
Hamond G E	Capt RN	**31**.262	a son
Hardacre H T		**12**.86	a sixth daughter
Hardacre	Lt RN	**14**.350	a daughter
Hardacre	Lt RN	**20**.255	a son, after a run of 8 daughters
Hartwell Francis	Sir	**29**.511	a daughter
Hawkey Charles	Capt RN	**33**.351	a daughter
Hawtayne	Capt RN	**21**.264	a daughter
Hayes	Capt RN	**28**.512	a daughter
Heathcote H	Capt	**18**.267	a son
Heathcote H	Capt	**24**.252	a daughter
Heathcote Gilbert	Capt RN	**24**.514	a daughter
Heathcote H	Capt	**29**.263	a daughter

Hodder	Capt RN	14.511	a son
Hodgson Brian	Capt RN	19.86	a son
Hodgson	Capt RN	24.174	a son
Hodgson	Capt RN	27.514	a son
Honeyman	Capt RN	20.335	a son
Hood Samuel	Hon	30.175	a daughter
Hope Ann Johnstone	Lady	19.175	a son
Hope George	Capt	19.263	a son
Horton S	Capt RN	21.87	a daughter
Hoseason Thomas		19.263	a son
Houstoun John	Capt RN	20.493	a son
Humphreys	Capt RN	16.264	a son
Hunter J		27.351	a son
Hutcheson Alexander Copland		20.493	a son
Inman	Professor	24.514	a son
Inman James	Reverend	27.514	a son
Innes Alexander	Capt RN	29.439	a son
Jenkins	Capt RN	10.517	a son
Jenkins Henry	Capt RN	20.335	a daughter
Johnson J		18.83	a son
Johnson P		27.351	?
Johnstone C	Capt	23.264	a daughter
Johnstone James		27.514	a son
Jones	Capt RN, Hon	32.87	a son
Katon	Capt RN	12.511	a son
Katon	Capt RN	24.514	a son
Keith	Adm Lord	23.87	a daughter
Kennedy	Capt RN	21.351	a daughter
King Richard	Sir	19.351	a daughter
King Charles	Lt RN	25.174	at Gatty Head, Ireland, a son
King William	Capt RN	26.263	stillborn
King J		26.514	a son
Knowles Chas Henry	V Adm Sir	12.511	a daughter
Knowles Chas Henry	Adm Sir	24.351	a daughter
Lake	Capt RN	27.351	a daughter
Lambert Henry	Capt RN	28.176	a son
Lambeth	Capt RN	9.339	a son
Lamburne	Capt RN	26.350	a son
Lane	Mr	28.512	at Newtown, a daughter
Langford George	Capt RN	11.343	a son
Langford G	Capt RN	22.519	a son
Larkins Thomas	Capt HEIC	21.264	a daughter
Laughlin B W		30.521	a son
Lawrence	Mrs	19.175	a son
Lawrence John	Capt RN	26.178	a son
Lawrence John	Capt RN	30.175	a daughter
Lee J T		20.255	a son
Lee J T	Mrs	28.262	a daughter
Lillicrap	Capt RN	31.351	a daughter
Linzee S H	Capt	18.347	a daughter
Linzee S H	R Adm	28.352	a son
Long Lawson		28.262	a daughter

Loring Wentworth		22.175	a daughter
Loring	Capt RN	26.263	a son
Losack G	Capt RN	13.423	a son
Losack Woodley	Capt	23.175	a son
Louis Mathew		19.439	a daughter
Louis John	Capt Sir	20.493	a son
Lukin	Capt RN	7.364	a son
Lumley	Capt RN	29.87	a daughter
Lydiard	Capt RN	7.364	a son
Lynne Thomas	Lt	19.86	a son
Lysaght	Capt RN	33.86	a son
M'Cleverty	Major RM	21.86	a son
M'Cleverty	Major RM	24.85	a son
M'Coy Robert	Lt RN	27.437	a daughter
M'Dowald	Dr MD RN	27.264	a son
M'Kinley	Capt RN	23.519	a daughter
M'Kinley	Capt RN	34.88	a daughter
M'Leod	Capt	22.351	a daughter
Mainwaring	Capt RN	28.262	a son
Maitland F	Capt RN	14.511	a son
Malbon	Capt RN	23.87	a son
Malcolm Pultney	Capt	21.264	a son
Malcolm	R Adm	31.175	a son
Manby	Capt	24.514	a daughter
Markham	Capt Hon	9.165	a son
Markham J	Hon Mrs	14.261	a son
Markham	V Adm	24.514	a son
Marten	Capt RN	32.262	a son
Martin John		33.351	a son
Mason	Capt RN	16.175	at St John's Newfoundland, a son
Mason Francis	Capt RN	32.262	a daughter
Masters	Capt RN	24.85	a son
Maude	Capt RN	33.351	?
Meller Douglas	Capt RN	26.514	at Douglas IoM, 3 sons, all of whom died soon after birth
Mends	Capt RN	10.175	a daughter
Mends	Capt RN	22.264	a daughter
Mends	Capt RN	30.175	a son
Mends Robert	Capt RN	32.351	a daughter
Mitford Robert		21.264	a son
Money	Capt RN	23.349	a daughter
Mulgrave	Rt Hon Lord	20.493	a son
Mulgrave	Rt Hon Lord	22.352	a son
Murray G	Capt	9.339	a son
Murray Robert	Adm	31.87	a daughter, (survived 24hrs)
Nash	Capt RN	26.178	a son
Nash	Capt RN	29.439	a son
Nesbitt	Capt RN	28.176	a son
New	Capt RN	13.85	a daughter
New	Capt RN	26.350	at Chatham, a daughter
Niblett Harry		32.262	a son
Northesk	Countess	18.83	a son
Northesk	Countess	26.178	a daughter

Northesk	Countess	**29.263**	a son
O'Connor	Capt RN	**18.174**	a daughter
Ogilvey	Capt RN	**9.250**	a son
Ogilvey	Capt RN	**11.175**	a son
Oglesby	Mr	**28.262**	at Portsea, a son
Ommanney Henry	Capt	**19.351**	a daughter
Ommanney H M	Capt RN	**22.175**	a son
Ommanney J A	Capt RN	**22.175**	a daughter
Omman(n)ey H M	Capt RN	**25.352**	a son
Ommanney	Mr	**29.263**	a son
Ommanney	Capt RN	**30.521**	a daughter
Orde John	V Adm Sir	**9.497**	a daughter
Orde J	Adm Sir	**16.87**	a daughter
Osborne J		**33.351**	stillborn
Otway	Commiss	**10.175**	a son
Otway R W	Capt RN	**10.263**	a daughter
Otway R W	Capt RN	**14.86**	a daughter
Otway	Capt RN	**19.263**	a daughter
Otway P N	Capt RN	**22.264**	a daughter
Otway Walter	R Adm	**34.88**	a son
Paget Peter	Capt RN	**18.437**	a daughter
Paget	Capt RN, Hon	**20.166**	a daughter
Paget	Capt RN, Hon	**23.175**	a daughter
Paget	Capt RN, Hon	**26.178**	a son
Paget Charles	Mrs	**33.511**	a daughter
Panchen John		**28.262**	a son
Parker Hyde	Adm Sir	**9.87**	a son
Parker Hyde	Adm Sir	**14.262**	a daughter
Parker Peter	Capt	**22.440**	a son
Parker Peter	Capt Sir	**28.87**	a son
Parker William G	Sir	**29.174**	a son
Parker Peter	Sir	**31.175**	a son
Parkin	Dr	**29.351**	a son
Pascoe	Capt	**24.437**	on board the Hindostan, at sea a son
Paterson	Capt HEIC	**23.439**	a daughter
Paterson W	Capt RN	**26.514**	a son
Patterson	Capt RN	**20.423**	a son
Patterson	Capt RN	**24.174**	a son
Payne W		**32.262**	a son
Pellew E	Sir	**9.81**	a son
Pellew P	Capt RN	**25.174**	a son
Pellew	Capt RN	**31.438**	a son
Pierrepont	Capt RN	**9.423**	a son
Pierrepont C H	Capt Hon	**14.350**	a son
Pierrepont	Capt RN, Hon	**22.264**	a daughter
Pipon	Capt RN	**26.350**	at Jersey, a son
Pipon	Capt RN	**30.359**	at Jersey, a son
Pipon	Capt RN	**30.447**	at Guernsey, a son
Pole Charles	Adm Sir	**10.174**	a daughter
Pole Charles	V Adm Sir	**14.174**	a daughter
Popham Home	Sir	**11.87**	a daughter
Popham Home	Sir	**13.335**	a son
Popham Home	Sir	**20.255**	a son

Popham Home	Sir	22.519	a son (10th child)
Popham H	Capt RN, Sir	27.437	a son (11th child)
Power	Lt RN	27.174	at Havant, a son
Prevost	Capt	19.515	a daughter
Prevost	Capt RN	24.174	a son
Prevost	Capt RN	28.87	a daughter
Prevost	Capt RN	33.87	a son
Pritchard B D	Lt RN	25.439	a son
Pritchard	Lt RN	29.511	a son
Puget	Commiss	31.438	at Madras, a daughter
Purches	Lt RN	26.350	a son
Reid Charles Hope	Capt	33.86	a son
Robb	Capt RN	29.351	a daughter
Robertson R	Dr	21.444	a daughter
Roby	Capt RN	14.174	two daughters
Rodd John Tremayne	Capt	27.264	a son
Rolles	Capt RN	28.262	a son
Rolls	Capt RN	20.335	a son
Rooke	Capt RN	31.87	a son
Ross James	Capt RN	8.352	a daughter
Ross	Capt RN	12.165	a daughter
Russell	Capt RN	24.437	at Aberdeen, a son
Rye P	Capt RN	30.521	a daughter
Ryves George Fred.	Capt	24.514	a son
Saunders T	Capt HEIC	19.515	a son
Saunders	Capt RN	24.437	a daughter
Sayer	Capt RN	27.86	a daughter
Schomberg A W	Capt RN	10.517	a son
Schomberg	Capt RN	14.261	a daughter
Schomberg	Capt RN	22.519	a son
Schomberg Alexander	Capt	32.87	a son
Schomberg A	Capt	32.262	a son
Scott H M	Capt	8.520	a son
Scott M H	Capt RN	11.343	a son
Scott M H	Capt RN	21.87	a daughter
Scott H M	Capt RN	23.175	a son
Scott	Lt RM	30.175	a son
Scott	R Adm	33.264	a daughter
Scott	R Adm	34.176	a son
Searle T	Capt RN	17.520	a son
Searle Thomas	Capt RN	25.352	a daughter
Seppings R		18.174	a son and daughter
Serrel John	Capt	20.166	a daughter
Seward	Capt RN	13.335	a daughter
Seymour M	Capt Sir	25.351	a daughter
Shippard A		10.174	a son and daughter
Shirreff	Capt RN	32.438	a daughter
Simpson	Mr	15.351	Surgeon of the Arethusa, a son
Spear	Capt RN	25.85	at Yarmouth, a son
Spear R	Capt RN	27.437	a daughter
Spence	Capt RN	33.511	a son
Spencer R	Capt RN	33.440	a son
Spencer	Capt RN	36.86	at Leghorn, a son
Stanfell	Capt RN	28.352	a daughter
Stevens George H	Capt RN	12.511	a daughter

Stevens J	Capt	28.262	a daughter
Strachan Richard	V Adm	29.439	a son
Strachan Richard	V Adm Sir	32.87	a daughter
Swaine Spelman	Capt RN	20.493	a daughter
Swaine Spelman	Capt	26.350	a daughter
Territt William	Hon	25.85	at Bermuda, a daughter
Thompson Thomas B	RN, Sir	11.343	a son
Thompson T B	Sir	24.252	a son
Tobin	Capt RN	24.437	a daughter
Tomlinson Nicholas	Capt RN	25.174	a daughter
Tooley Ann	Mrs	21.175	a daughter
Torrington	Viscountess	33.511	a daughter
Torrington	Viscountess	36.518	a son
Torrington	Viscount	40.84	a son
Towry G H	Capt RN	10.263	a son
Towry	Capt RN	13.423	a daughter
Tremenheere	Capt RM	11.87	a son
Trickey	Lt	9.423	a son
Tucker Benjamin		22.351	a son
Tucker Joseph		27.514	a son
Upton	Capt RN	16.87	a daughter
Upton	Capt RN	28.176	at Cork, a daughter
Vansittart Henry	Capt RN	25.439	a son
Wainwright	Capt RN	28.87	a son
Wainwright	Capt RN	30.175	a daughter
Walker	Capt RN	17.439	a daughter
Walker	Capt RN	28.512	a son
Walton Jacob	Capt	24.252	a son
Warren	Capt RN	31.175	at Sandwich, a daughter
Watkins	Capt RN	14.174	a son
Webley	Capt RN	27.514	a daughter
Wells F L	Capt RM	26.438	a son
Western	Capt RN	14.350	a daughter
Western	R Adm	33.86	a son
Whitby	Capt RN	10.175	a daughter
Whyte	Capt RN	15.440	a son
Williamson Joseph		28.87	stillborn son
Wilson	R Adm	11.87	a daughter
Wilson	Capt RN	17.439	a son
Wilson	Adm	18.519	a son
Wise	Capt RN	28.176	a son
Wiseman W S	Capt RN, Sir	29.511	at Bombay, a son
Woolley Isaac	Capt RN	23.439	a son
Woolward	Lt RN	28.351	a son
Worth John	Capt RN	26.514	a daughter
Yarwood S		25.351	a daughter
Yorke Joseph S	Capt Sir	13.423	a son
Yorke Joseph S	R Adm Sir	26.514	a daughter
Young	Capt RN	9.250	a son
Young J	Capt	11.493	a son
Young J	Capt RN	16.175	a daughter
Young W	Capt RN	25.85	a son

| **Young W** | Capt | **27**.514 | a son (13th child) |
| **Younghusband** | Capt HEIC | **24**.514 | a daughter |

MARRIAGES

Abdy	Capt RN	20.255	
Abdy Charlotte Ann	Miss	20.493	
Abdy Catherine Mary	Miss	30.447	
Aberdour James	Capt RN	27.438	
Achorly	Lt RM	8.439	
Ackland Robert		38.87	
Adam James		22.520	at Maryton, Exeter
Adams E	Miss	34.351	
Adamson Abraham	Capt	25.86	
Aikman Anne Hunter	Miss	25.440	
Aitken	Mr (Surgeon)	23.519	
Albrecht	Miss	18.437	at Bath
Alcock	Capt RN	30.87	
Alcott	Miss	30.359	at Portsmouth
Aldham	Capt RN	16.264	
Aldred	Miss	33.176	of Monmouth
Aldridge	Miss	27.264	by special licence
Alexander	Lt RM	7.532	
Alexander	Capt RN	27.264	
Alexander N	Capt RN	34.440	at Cork
Allen John Carter	Adm	2.171	
Allen	Miss	11.263	at Plymouth
Allen	Capt RN	25.513	at Gibraltar
		26.86	
Allen Thomas		27.514	
Anderson	Capt	4.444	
		4.516	
Anderson	Miss	14.511	at Plymouth
Anderson A	Lt RM	16.175	
Anderson	Lt Col RM	19.176	at Kilkeedy, Limerick
Anderson Elizabeth	Miss	19.439	
Anderson Archibald		26.178	
Anderson	Surgeon RN	32.263	at Plymouth
Andover	Viscountess	15.351	
Andrew Unity	Miss	19.263	
Andrews George	Capt RN	24.85	
Anthony G	Capt	21.444	
Anthony	Miss	33.511	at Portsea
Apperley Frances	Miss	7.364	
Appleby J M	Miss	24.85	
Argles George	Capt RN	30.264	
Armstrong C	Miss	25.263	
Armstrong Henrietta	Miss	25.263	at Bombay
Armstrong Harriett	Miss	25.513	at Bombay
Arnold Jane	Miss	22.440	
Arnold	Lt RN	26.514	
Arnold	Miss	28.352	of Portsea, at St Martin's in the Fields
Arnold Charlotte	Miss	30.175	
Arrow J J	Lt RN	29.174	
Arundel Julianna	the Hon	34.439	daughter of the late Lord A.
Ashelby	Mr (Surgeon)	6.84	
Ashford	Mr	12.255	at Sherborne
Askew	Capt	24.438	at Maddron, Cornwall
Aste	Miss	20.255	at Chippenham
Atkins	Lt RN	8.352	

Atkinson Joseph		25.86	at St Peter's, Dublin
Atkinson Jane	Miss	30.264	
Atkinson William	Reverend	33.351	
Atkinson	Miss	35.175	at Portland Place
Austen F W	Capt	16.175	
Ayde	Capt RN	24.351	
Aylmer	V Adm	22.440	
Aylward Elizabeth C	Miss	21.176	
Ayres A	Miss	24.351	
Ayscough	Miss	22.175	of Southampton at Chiswick
Ayscough John	Capt RN	26.515	
Babington T G		32.176	
Bacon Ann	Miss	26.515	
Bagnell J C	Lt RM	20.255	
Bagnell	Mrs	31.438	at Chippenham
Baikie Cecilia Mary	Miss	28.439	
Bailey Mary Jane	Miss	26.514	
Bailey S	Miss	27.351	
Bailey Mary Ann	Miss	31.438	
Bailey H W	Lt RN	33.511	
Baker Jane	Miss	34.352	
Baldy	Miss	26.178	at Portsmouth
Balfour R	Lt RN	16.88	
Ball Henry Lidgbird	Capt RN	7.532	
Ball Anne Maria	Miss	24.85	
Ball Henry Lidgbird	Capt RN	24.85	
Ball	Miss	31.87	at Falmouth
Ballard Volant V	Capt RN	26.264	
Baillie Alex. F	Capt RN	10.175	
Baillie James		28.176	
		28.262	
Baines Elizabeth J	Miss	6.434	
Balderston S	Miss	8.520	
Banks	Miss	29.439	at Ryde
Banks W H		31.511	
Banks W H		32.351	
Banks Elizabeth	Miss	33.264	
Banks John	Capt RN	33.264	
Barber Clare F	Miss	14.174	
Barber W B	Reverend	25.85	
Barclay	Miss	28.176	at St Mary-le-bone Ch
Barclay R H	Capt RN	32.263	
Barfoot	Lt	34.439	2nd or Queen's Regmt
Barlow Frances H	Miss	26.351	
Barnard William	Capt HEIC	25.439	
Barnard	Lt RN	26.264	at Plymouth
Barnes	Lt RN	25.263	
Barnes	Miss	31.175	at Surry Place, Kent Rd
Barnett	Miss	25.263	of Fratton
Barney	Mr	19.176	at Fareham
Barns	Miss	14.511	of Portsmouth
Barr Margaret	Miss	6.348	
Barrett	Capt	25.263	
Barrow	Miss	27.514	at Plymouth
Bartlett	Mr	27.175	of Portsmouth

Barton	Miss	4.527	
Barton	Miss	11.263	at Plymouth
Barton Elizabeth	Miss	24.515	
Barton James	Lt RN	27.264	
Basden	Capt	21.519	
Bashford	Capt RN	23.87	at Birkenhead Priory
Baskerville	Miss	32.439	of Hurst Castle, IoW
Bate Ann	Miss	25.86	
Bateman	Capt RN	22.88	
Bateman	Lt RN	33.511	
Bateman Amelia Anne	Miss	34.176	
Bathurst Walter	Capt	19.176	
Bayley Rosa Maria	Miss	28.513	
Bayly	Lt RN	29.511	
Bayly	Miss	29.511	
Baynes Robert	Reverend	26.514	at Cape of Good Hope
Baynton	Capt RN	22.175	
Bazely Henry	Capt	5.96	
Beamish William		32.263	
Beaufort F	Capt RN	28.513	
Beaver	Capt RN	4.347	
Beaver Margaret	Miss	32.351	
Becher Anne	Miss	39.343	
Bechinal A	Miss	12.255	
Beck Fanny	Miss	35.263	
Beckitt	Lt RN	33.351	
Bedford	Lt RN	14.511	of Ryl Hosp Greenwich
Bedford	Capt	19.176	
Bedford James Gover	Reverend	27.438	of Avington, Hants at St Andrew's Holborn
Belcher Nathaniel	RN	9.423	
Bell Elinor	Miss	26.87	
Bell G	Capt	31.87	
Bellamy G	Mr	3.516	
Benfield	Miss	29.263	
Bennamore S	Miss	33.176	at Gibraltar
Bennett	Miss	16.88	at Kingston Church
Bennett A	Miss	19.86	
Bennett Charles Cowper		23.440	
Bennett	Capt RN, Hon	26.264	
Bennett William	Capt RN	33.176	
Bennett		33.511	formerly of Bengal
Bennicke	Mrs	31.175	at Liskeard
Bentham M	Miss	10.517	
Bentham	Miss	18.437	at Minster, Sheppy
Bentinck William	Capt RN	8.439	
Bentinck Harriet	Miss	11.343	
Benyon	Miss	29.352	at St George's, Hanover Sq.
Beresford J P	Capt RN	21.519	by special licence
Beresford John	R Adm Sir	34.176	
Berkeley Georginia	Miss	25.439	
Berkeley Mary	Miss	28.87	
Berkley	Miss	19.86	at Halifax
Bessant	Miss	27.175	of Portsea
Bettesworth	Lt RN	7.532	
Bettesworth B	Miss	12.431	

Bettesworth	Miss	13.85	
Bettesworth	Capt RN	18.347	
Bevan	Major	13.85	of 28th Regmt of Foot
Bicknell M A	Miss	27.438	
Biddulph Frances A	Miss	23.519	
Biddulph F P	Miss	33.87	
Biden Christopher	of HEIC	40.164	
Bidwell Sarah	Miss	27.86	
Bignell	Miss	32.263	at Plymouth
Bignell George	Capt RN	35.516	
Bilbie F		8.352	at Calcutta
Binford Thomas		27.86	
Bingham A B	Capt RN	29.263	
Birchall	Capt RN	16.88	
Bishop	Lt RN	17.176	at Newfoundland
Bishop	Lt	18.174	at St John's, Newfoundland
Blachford Elizabeth	Miss	11.175	
Black Susanna	Miss	26.87	
Blackler	Lt RN	26.178	at Stoke Ch, Plymouth
Blackwell	Miss	20.166	of Packham, Suffolk
Blackwood Henry	Capt RN	2.82	
Blackwood Henry	Capt RN, Hon	9.423	
Blake Honoria	Miss	23.350	
Blake John Charles		28.513	
Blakeney J	Lt	18.347	in Newfoundland
Blamborough	Miss	34.439	
Blancoe Frances D	Miss	25.263	
Blanter	Miss	12.165	at Plymouth
Blaxton	Miss	27.351	
Blewett	Miss	25.352	of Stonehouse
Bligh Anne C	Miss	2.82	
Bligh	V Adm	4.168	
Bligh John	Capt RN	22.176	
Blight	Miss	25.352	of Plymouth
Bluett	Miss	25.174	of East Stonehouse
Bluett Buckland S	Capt RN	29.263	
Bodens Anna G	Miss	18.174	
Boger	Miss	1.446	
Boger	Mrs	16.264	
Bolton	Mr	6.348	at Mary-le-bone Church
Bolton Catherine	Miss	9.423	
Bolton William	Capt RN, Sir	9.423	
Bonamy	Miss	26.515	of Portsmouth
Bone F		28.438	
Bonham	Capt HEIC	8.439	
Bonnycastle	Miss	29.263	of Woolwich
Bonthrone Eleanor	Miss	26.178	
Boorn	Mrs	24.263	at Romsey
Booth George		22.175	
Booth Elizabeth A	Miss	26.263	
Bouchier Charlotte	Mrs	23.264	
Bourchier Ellen	Miss	33.351	
Bourgho John A de	Sir	19.439	
Bourgoyne	Miss	33.87	
Bourke N A		22.520	
Bowden Ann	Miss	10.350	of Portsea

Bowden	Lt RM	11.87	
Bowden N	Capt RN	33.511	
Bowdler T		16.264	
Bowen C	Lt	11.493	
Bowers M A	Miss	8.87	
Bowker	Lt RN	6.172	
Bowyer George	Sir	20.423	
Bowyer	Miss	32.511	at Titchfield
Boxald	Miss	34.352	of Arundel
Boyard Caroline	Miss	26.87	
Boyce	Mr (Sgn RN)	34.440	
Boys	Miss	2.263	
Bradby	Mrs	19.352	of Catisfield, Hants
Bradby	Capt	20.493	
Bradby Mary Allen	Miss	27.438	
Braddyll	Miss	30.447	at Hampton
Bradley W H	Lt RN	25.263	
Bradshaw	Mr	10.438	
Braine Mary	Miss	34.88	
Brall F	Miss	8.352	
Brathwaite Eliza	Miss	21.352	
Brawn Francis S		24.438	
Breedon	Miss	15.87	
Bremer Gordon	Capt RN	25.352	
Brenton Edward	Capt RN	9.339	
Brett	Capt RN	3.516	
Bridgeman George	Reverend Hon	22.175	
Bridgman Mary-Ann	Miss	32.263	
Bridgman Alice	Miss	33.351	
Bridgman Orlando	the Hon	38.88	
Briggs T W	Reverend	29.511	
Briggs J A	Capt HEIC	33.351	at Calcutta
Bright Anna M	Miss	27.264	
Brightwell E	Miss	20.80	
Brinson R		25.174	
Brisac D	Lt RM	31.87	at St John's, Newfoundland
Brisbain	Capt	3.516	
Bristow Fanny	Miss	24.174	
		24.352	
Britton	Lt RM	17.520	
Bromley R		14.350	
Bromley Samuel		22.88	
Brooke	Miss	23.519	of Cheshire
Broughton	Capt RN	8.439	
Broughton Jemima	Miss	8.439	
Brown	Miss	6.84	of London
Brown Ann	Lady	16.175	
Brown	Mr	22.88	at Deal
Brown	Miss	23.350	at Kinsale
Brown Ann	Miss	29.263	
Brown Caroline G	Miss	34.440	
Browne Edward W	Capt	2.263	
Browne	Miss	4.526	
Browne	Miss	15.440	
Browne P		25.440	
Browne Charlotte	Miss	27.264	

Bruce Charlotte	Lady	1.347	
Bruce	Miss	14.262	at Fareham
Bruce Michael		40.164	
Bruff Peter Schuyler		26.87	
Bryan C	Reverend	31.438	
Bryant	Miss	9.423	of Newport, Essex
Bryer Elizabeth	Miss	25.85	
Buckle	Capt RN	1.261	
Buckle	Miss	9.165	
Buckle Matthew		9.165	
Buckle	Mr	27.351	of Ryde, IoW
Buckler Ann	Miss	33.511	
Bucknor	Miss	30.447	at Clewer Church
Budd Henry Hayward	Lt RN	21.264	
Bugler Lucinda	Miss	25.513	at St John's, Newfoundland
Bull John	Capt	1.540	
Buller	Miss	19.439	by special licence
Buller William		34.439	
Bulley C	Miss	6.259	
Bulley George	Capt RN	34.440	
Bullmore Timothy		31.438	
Bullock Mary	Miss	12.86	
Bullock Sarah	Miss	13.85	
Bullock	Miss	13.246	
Bunce Mary	Miss	38.88	
Bunn Edward Thomas		27.264	at Calcutta
Burchett Clarissa	Miss	27.264	
Burdett George	Capt RN	8.176	
Burdett	Capt RN	15.440	
Burgess	Miss	26.514	at Cape of Good Hope
Burke John	Lt	21.444	of Westmeath Militia
Burlton Sarah	Miss	23.440	
Burn	Mrs	32.176	widow of Capt John Burn RN
Burnaby William	Capt RN, Sir	36.86	at Bermuda
Burne Daniel		18.267	at St John's, Newfoundland
Burnett	Miss	25.263	of Portsmouth
Burnett Eliza	Miss	27.175	
Burney C P	Reverend	25.86	of Merton College, Oxford
Burney George		27.175	
Burney	Capt	38.88	of the 44th Regmt
Burridge	Miss	26.351	of Creech St Michael, Portsmouth
Burt	Miss	3.420	
Burton	Lady	28.176	
		28.262	
Burton Thomas	Capt RN	32.263	
Burton G	Capt RN	34.439	
Bushby Mary	Miss	9.165	
Bushby John	Capt RN	9.165	
Bushby	Mrs	28.438	
Bussell W	Reverend	7.452	
Butcher E	Miss	3.331	
Butler	Miss	8.352	at Windlesham
Butler Thomas	Capt HEIC	9.339	
Butler	Miss	19.86	at Weymouth
Butler G	Lt RN	34.88	

Butler	Miss	36.86	of Salisbury
Butter	Capt	28.439	Wilts Militia at Guernsey
Butterfield	Capt RN	12.431	
By	Lt	6.434	Royal Engineers
Byam William Henry	Capt RN	30.447	
Byland Count	Lt Col	8.87	of Hompesch's Regmt of Dragoons
Byles	Mr	27.351	at Portsea
Byng Henry Dilkes	Capt RN	24.514	at Halifax, Nova Scotia
Byng George	Capt RN	26.351	
Byron	Capt RN	6.259	
Cadogan G	Capt RN	23.350	
Cairns James	Doctor RN	8.176	
Caldwell Charles A		20.493	
Caledon	Rt Hon Lord	26.438	
Callbeck Eliza	Miss	12.341	
Camell Robert		6.172	
Cameron	Miss	32.87	at Halifax, Nova Scotia
		32.262	
Cameron Archibald	Capt HEIC	32.351	
Campbell	Miss	1.347	
Campbell Robert	Capt RN	12.511	
Campbell E	Miss	13.164	
Campbell	R Adm	13.164	
Campbell	Mrs	19.352	at Milton House, Scotland
Campbell Donald	Capt RN	19.439	
Campbell Laura	Miss	34.440	
Camsell	Miss	33.511	of Wovill
Canaway William		26.264	
Cannaway	Miss	23.511	of Portsmouth Dockyard
Cannon	Miss	9.165	of Middle Deal
Cant	Miss	2.448	
Cantwell Harriet	Miss	30.359	
		30.447	
Capel T B	RN, Hon	35.440	
Carey	Miss	34.176	of Portsea
Carlton	Miss	6.348	at Mary-le-bone Church
Carlyon	Miss	22.520	of Trogrehan, Cornwall
Carmichel	Lt	32.262	104th Regmt at Prince Edward's Island, North America
Carnac Anna Maria	Miss	20.166	
Carnac E Rivett	Miss	23.519	
Carnegie Mary		23.175	eldest daughter of the Earl of Northesk, by special licence
Carpenter	Mr	24.175	at Honiton
Carpenter	Mrs	33.511	
Carpenter Eliza	Miss	34.440	late of Newfoundland
Carr	Miss	5.280	
Carre Elizabeth	Miss	25.174	
Carroll William F	Capt RN	30.175	
Carruthers	Lt RM	1.261	
Carswell A	Miss	28.513	
Carter	Miss	7.532	of Portsea
Carter S	Miss	8.439	

Carter	Capt RM	14.511	
Carter	Capt RN	15.87	
Carter W	Mr	19.439	
Carter	Miss	23.519	of Portsea (formerly of Itchenor)
Carter Elizabeth	Miss	29.87	
Carter Jane	Miss	33.176	
Carteret M	Miss	13.504	
Carthew	Capt RN	27.514	at Antigua
Carthew	Mrs	31.438	
Carthew	Capt RN	32.511	at Bath
Case Harriet	Miss	4.347	
Casey	Lt RN	20.423	
Casey David O'Brien		27.438	at Cork
Cassamajor Amelia	Miss	24.85	at Madras
Cator Bertie	Capt RN	35.175	
Causton	Miss	5.375	of Cornhill, London
Cazal	Miss	20.423	of Exeter, married at Gretna Green
Chads	Miss	19.176	at Fareham
Chads Henry Ducie	Capt RN	34.511	
Chalmers Charles Wm	Capt Sir	34.176	
Chamberlaine	Miss	8.439	
Chambers David	Lt RN	11.421	
Champion S		13.504	at Jersey
Champion Eliza	Miss	29.439	
Champion John Hyde		34.440	at Jersey
Charlotte	HRH Princess	35.439	
Charlton W	Capt RN	12.431	
Charlton	Mrs	25.85	(nee Caulfield) of Bath
Charlton John		26.263	
Charlton	Mrs	26.515	widow of Wm Charlton of HM Frigate Garland
Charrett	Miss	32.262	at Portsmouth
Chase Joseph		17.520	
Chechagoff	R Adm	2.547	of the Russian Navy
Chetham	Capt RN	24.85	
Chetwynd Lucy H	Miss	22.88	
Chevers F M		25.440	
Cholwich	Miss	1.261	
Chown	Miss	24.515	of Plymouth
Christian Mary	Miss	8.87	
Christian	Capt RN	19.263	
Christiana Mary	Mrs	24.438	at Bombay
Christie	Mr	4.347	
Christie Alexander		25.86	of 5th Dragoon Guards
Christie Archibald		28.513	
Christy William		26.178	
Chubb Harriet	Miss	20.493	
Churchill Eliza Ann	Miss	34.511	
Churchill Ann	Miss	35.263	
Clanricarde	Marchioness of	29.439	by special licence
Clanwilliam	Earl of	14.262	
Clarence	Duke of	40.69	
Clark	Lt RN	9.497	
Clark Mary	Miss	28.513	
Clarke	Miss	3.331	

Clarke W		19.176	
Clarke	Capt RM	19.439	at Bath
Clarke Maria Jane	Miss	24.514	at Halifax, Nova Scotia
Clavell	Lt RN	6.259	
Clayton M	Miss	27.86	
Cleather	Miss	10.263	of Plymouth
Clement	Capt RN	26.351	at Chawton
Cleveland Sarah E	Miss	30.447	
Cleverton Mary Ann	Mrs	28.439	
Clifton Marshall W		26.87	
Cliverton	Mr	15.87	
Cochet John	Capt RN	26.86	
Cochrane	Miss	24.352	at Mary-le-bone
Cochrane	Capt RN	27.86	
Cochrane Basil	Hon	28.176	
Cock James	Capt	26.178	
Cockburn	Miss	10.175	of Jamaica
Cockrell Elizabeth	Miss	26.515	
Cocks Margaretta S	Miss	8.439	
Cocks Maria	Miss	25.439	
Codd	Lt RN	6.84	
Codrington	Capt RN	9.81	
Coetlogan Charlotte de	Miss	2.448	
Coffin Isaac	V Adm Sir	25.352	now known as Sir Isaac Coffin Greenly
Coker John		26.264	
Colby	Capt RN	15.440	
Cole Martin	Lt RN	28.352	
Cole John	Reverend	30.359	
Cole Christopher	Capt Sir	33.440	
Cole	Miss	34.88	of Waltham
Cole G H		34.351	
Cole William John	Lt RN	40.332	
Coleman W		32.351	
Coles John	Reverend	30.447	
Colley Augustus K	Lt RM	15.87	
Colley Edward		27.175	at Curacoa
Collier	Lt RN	17.352	
Collier	Mrs	27.351	of Portsea
Collingwood Sarah	Miss	35.516	
Collins John	of HEIC	19.263	
Collins E		22.520	
Collins John		30.522	
Collins R		34.352	
Collins Anne	Miss	35.352	
Colman G A		28.513	
Columbine Edward H	Capt RN	6.84	
Comben Jane	Miss	33.351	
Compton William		2.547	the bride given away by Lord Nelson
Comyn H	Reverend	32.262	
Connell	Miss	19.352	
Cook	Miss	18.83	of Greenwich
Cooke Georgiana	Miss	4.444	
Cooke	Miss	19.352	at Minster, Kent
Coombe William M	Major RM	28.176	

Constable	Mrs	25.263	at Kingston, Portsea
Conyers	Miss	26.264	of Copped-hall, Essex
Cooke Christopher		24.85	
Cooke Elizabeth	Miss	33.176	
Cookesley	Capt RN	22.352	at Anthony, Tor Point
Coomer	Lt RN	27.86	
Cooper J		13.246	
Cooper	Miss	19.176	of Cooper-hill
Coote	Miss	22.176	at St John's, Newfoundland
Cormack Elizabeth M	Miss	24.263	
Cormack	Miss	26.350	of Liverpool
Corne	Capt RN	7.532	
Corne	Mrs	25.439	
Cornwall	Miss	12.431	
Coryton Fidelia	Miss	23.439	
Cosser Agnes	Miss	32.263	
Costin	Mrs	15.440	
Cotton Arabella A	Miss	6.84	
Coul	Miss	31.175	of Ashgrove
Countess Mary	Miss	35.516	
Court Charles	Capt HEIC	24.514	
Coward Samuel	Capt	27.264	
Cowie	Miss	17.520	
Cox	Miss	9.339	
Cox Maria	Mrs	24.263	at Bombay
Cox	Miss	26.264	of Portsea
Crab	Miss	20.80	of Stonehouse, by special licence
		20.167	disavowal of previous entry
Crabb Arabella S	Miss	26.264	
Crabtree	Miss	25.513	of Witton, Norfolk
Cragge	Miss	18.519	
Craig Caroline	Miss	22.520	
Craig	Miss	33.351	at Finsbury
Crane	Miss	28.87	of Ryde, IoW
Cranstoun	Rt Hon Lord	18.347	at St Christopher's
Crawford	Capt RN	12.165	
Crawford Peter	Capt RN	32.263	
Crawford James C	Capt RN	35.440	at Amhendening
Cresswell	Capt RM	29.87	
Crichton	Miss	27.175	at St Martin's in the Fields
Croft	Capt RN	13.335	
Croft	Mrs	26.87	widow of J Croft RN
Crofton	Lt RM	24.515	at Woolwich
Crosier	Capt	8.352	
Cross Arabella	Miss	6.516	
Cross	Miss	16.88	of Bath
Crouch Mary	Miss	24.351	
Crouch E T	Lt RN	32.511	
Crown G F		19.352	
Cremer	Miss	3.516	
Crutchley Catherine	Miss	32.263	
Culley S	Miss	33.511	
Cullum Mary Ann	Miss	24.263	
Cumberland	Capt RN	3.420	
Cuming Caroline	Miss	29.263	

Cumming Sarah Ann	Miss	28.439	
Cunningham	Mr	19.263	at Portsmouth
Curry Ann	Miss	6.84	
Curry Richard	Capt RN	11.175	
Curry Jane	Miss	24.85	
Curtis	Capt RN	25.513	at Widley, Hants
Cuthbert	Capt RN	9.87	
Dacres	Miss	13.85	
Dacres	Capt RN	23.440	
Dacres Martha M	Miss	30.175	
Daintry Mary	Miss	27.514	
Dale	Miss	11.175	of Chelsea
Dallas Marrianne	Miss	21.264	
Dallas	Miss	26.515	at Mary-le-bone Church
Dalrymple Hugh	Sir	3.420	
Dalrymple J	Miss	13.85	
Dalrymple Arabella	Miss	23.440	
Dalrymple Charlotte	Miss	35.440	
Danford Elizabeth	Miss	38.88	
Daniels	Miss	25.174	of Bristol, at Plymouth
Darwin Harriet	Miss	26.515	
Dashwood	Capt RN	2.547	
Dashwood Caroline M	Miss	29.511	
D'Auvergne Mary A	Miss	34.88	
Davenant	Miss	25.263	at Kinterbury Lodge, Berks
Davenport	Mr	16.352	
Davidson	Miss	12.431	
Davie	Capt RN	33.176	
		33.351	
Davies W A		26.178	
Davies Henry	Lt RN	28.176	
Davies	Miss	32.262	
Davis Richard L		11.87	
Davis	Mr	18.519	
Davis	Miss	24.85	of Printing House Square
Davis Thomas		27.86	
Davison	Miss	8.520	of Chatham
Davison	Lt RN	25.174	
Day	Miss	24.514	of Portsea
Day John		28.513	
Day	Lt RM	31.438	of Chippenham
Dealty Jane	Miss	33.511	
Dean E	Miss	12.165	
Dean	Miss	24.85	
Dean Jemima	Miss	32.263	
Deans James	Capt RN	19.439	
Deare E	Miss	15.264	
Debaufre	Miss	11.493	
De Courcy	Hon Miss	2.547	
De Courcy Michael	Lt Hon	5.280	
De Courcy Ann	Miss	27.514	
De Courcy Mary	Hon	32.263	
Decourdoux George	Lt RN	22.440	
De L'Isle	Miss	5.280	of Salcombe, Devon
Denford C	Lt RM	14.511	

Dennis E S	Miss	34.351	
Denny Rebecca	Miss	6.348	
Denoon	Mrs	16.175	
Dent Frances	Miss	21.444	
Dent	Miss	24.514	
Denton	Mrs	20.493	at St George's, Hanover Sq.
Desborough	Col RM	10.517	
Dewsnap Eliza	Miss	26.514	of Woodstock, Oxon at Greenwich
Dicken John			see Temple, John
Dickens	Capt	27.514	of Southampton
Dickinson Harriet	Miss	26.264	
Dickson	V Adm	2.644	
Dickson W	Mrs	12.165	
Dickson D J H	Doctor	27.174	
Didham	Mr	34.439	at Humbledon
Digby	Capt RN	15.351	
Dilkes	Capt	12.255	
Dillon	Miss	20.80	of Penryn, at Batheaick Church, Bath
Dillon Louisa	Miss	27.438	
Dix Harriet	Miss	18.347	at Jersey
Dixon	Miss	24.438	of Newcastle
Dixon Manley	R Adm	25.439	
Dixon Sarah	Miss	29.511	
Dobell Amelia	Miss	25.440	
Dobree Eliza	Miss	28.439	at Guernsey
Domett	Miss	14.262	
Donnelly Jane	Miss	35.352	at Brussels
Doo S	Miss	1.174	
Douglas Howard	Lt RA	2.263	
Douglas Stair	Capt RN	8.87	
Douglas M	Miss	10.87	
Douglas Ann Irwin	Miss	19.439	
Douglas	Miss	20.423	at St George's, Hanover Sq.
Douglas Catherine	Miss	20.493	
Douglas	Miss	22.520	by special licence at Cumberland Place
Douglas A L	Miss	24.351	
Douglas Caroline L	Hon	24.438	
Douglas Henry		25.513	
Douglas Grace Mary	Miss	26.264	
Douglas W H	Lt RN	26.514	
Douglass	Miss	6.84	of Portsea
Doun	Miss	27.86	at Clist Hinton
Dove Piercy	Lt RN	1.347	
Dowdney	Miss	27.264	
Dowers William	Capt RN	25.513	at St Vincent's
Dowers	Miss	30.359	at Deal
Dowling Sarah	Miss	34.176	
Down	Capt HEIC	7.364	
Down Edward A	Capt RN	34.512	
Downer	Miss	24.515	late of Portsmouth Theatre
Downer Thomas		28.513	at St John's, Newfoundland
Downman	Capt RN	9.497	
Drake	Miss	10.517	

Driffield	Lt Col RM	2.82	
Drummond	Capt RN	5.464	
Drummond	Miss	9.339	by special licence
Drummond John		35.352	
Drury George V	of HEIC	18.519	
Dryden	Mr (Sgn RN)	26.87	
Dublin Caroline		34.511	2nd dau of the Archbishop
Duckworth	Miss	10.517	of Stoke, Plymouth
Duckworth J T	V Adm Sir	19.439	by special licence
Duddington	R Adm	8.520	
Duff	Mrs	11.493	of Richmond
Duff Sophia-H	Miss	25.85	might be 2nd marriage, first to 'Tobin'
Duff Richard	Capt RN	34.511	
Duggin	Miss	17.176	of St John's, Newfoundland
Duggin	Miss	18.174	at St John's, Newfoundland
Dumaresq	Capt	12.511	
Dumaresq Philip	Capt RN	32.176	at Jersey
Dunbar James	Capt Sir	31.175	
Duncan	Miss	3.420	
Duncan A	Miss	12.165	
Duncan Henrietta	Hon	12.511	
Duncan	Lord Viscount	13.85	
Dundas Anne	Miss	2.263	
Dundas	Capt RN	4.526	
Dundas Janet	Miss	19.439	
Dundas Maria	Miss	24.86	at Bombay
Dunn	Capt RN	25.352	at Teigngrace Church
Dunn D	Capt RN	30.175	
Dunn Pascoe	Lt RN	30.359	
Dunne	Capt RN	25.174	at Teigngrace Church
Dunsford William		24.262	
Dunstable	Miss	9.165	
Dunstone Peggy	Miss	28.438	
Durham	Capt RN	1.347	
Dutton Thomas	Lt RN	21.176	
Dutton T B	Lt RN	34.351	
Dyer Anne-Innes	Miss	32.263	
Earl	Miss	25.513	at Edinborough
Eastham Lucretia	Miss	32.263	
Eckford A	Lt	9.251	
Eden Thomas		24.86	at Colombo
Eden Drea	Miss	27.264	by special licence
Edgar Maria	Miss	12.511	
Edgecombe Martha	Miss	8.352	of Portsea
Edgecumbe Priscilla	Miss	21.176	
Edison John		8.87	
Edney	Miss	11.493	of Portsea
Edwards J	Capt RN	1.174	
Edwards Richard	Lt Col	10.87	Royal Caernarvonshire Militia
Edwards	Capt RN	14.262	at Hastings
Edwards	Miss	26.178	of Haslar
Edwards John	Lt RN	26.350	
Edwards S	Miss	27.438	
Edwards	Miss	28.263	of Tottenham, at Hoddesdon

Egan	Miss	26.264	at Jersey
Egerton	Lt Col	22.520	of 44th Regmt
Eggleston	Miss	4.444	
		4.516	
Elcock Mary Ann	Miss	29.174	
Elers	Lt RN	17.176	at Alverstoke
Ellary	Lt RN	27.175	at Weymouth
Ellers	Mrs	34.88	
Ellerton John Fred.		37.85	at Calcutta
Elliot	Miss	4.347	
Elliot George	Hon	24.438	at Calcutta
Elliot	Miss	38.87	of Kingsand
Elliott J E	Hon	24.85	at Madras
Elliott Thomas		25.513	of St John's, Newfoundland
Elliott Harriott	Miss	29.352	at Cronstadt, Russia
Ellis George	MP	6.434	
Ellis Henry William	Lt RM	32.263	
Ellison Esther	Miss	21.519	
Ellison	Miss	26.87	at Bangalore
Ellison William	Lt RN	35.86	
Elms	Miss	23.519	at Stoke Ch, Plymouth
Elphinstone	Capt	5.187	
Elphinstone	Miss	21.87	eldest daughter of the Hon WF Elphinstone
Elwin T N		26.438	
Emily	Miss	30.87	of Hardway
Epworth	Miss	12.255	
Erskine Henrietta	Miss	27.438	by special licence
Essex	Miss	30.175	
Euston	Earl of	28.87	at Lisbon
Evans	Lt RN	25.263	
Evans David	Reverend	30.175	
Eveleigh	Miss	3.156	
Ewright J		25.440	
Exley M	Miss	23.519	
Eyles J	Capt RN, Sir	12.255	
Eyre George	Capt	4.444	
Fabian	Capt RN	10.517	
Fairfax	Miss	12.86	at Edinburgh
Falconer	Lt RN	14.350	
Falkner Mary E	Miss	28.176	
Fanshawe	Miss	19.176	
Fanshawe Mary	Miss	22.88	
Fanshawe	Capt RN	23.439	
Farbrace	Miss	13.85	
Farquhar James		23.175	
Farquharson Cath.	Miss	2.171	
Farrer Spurgeon		21.351	
Farrington	Capt RA	24.85	
Faten P	Miss	30.522	
Faulknor Augustus	Reverend	3.240	
Fegan Richard	Lt RN	29.439	
Fellowes E	Capt RN	29.352	
Fellowes J	Capt RN	30.447	
Ferguson G	Capt RN	27.514	

Fergusson	Major	12.511	Ayrshire Militia
Ferris	Capt	13.423	of East India Service
Ferris T B		25.439	of Coldstream Guards
		26.87	
Ferris	Capt RN	26.86	
Ferritt William	Hon	23.349	at Bermuda
Field	Miss	25.174	of Castle Farm, near Plymouth
Fielding Charles	Capt RN	11.421	
Fielding Augusta	Miss	29.263	
Figg Ann	Miss	27.438	
Finch W	Lt RN	27.351	
Finling Charles	Capt RN	13.85	
Finnimore Thomas	Lt RN	25.174	
Fisher	Lt	23.519	at Bermuda
Fisher	Capt RN	23.519	
Fisher Maria	Miss	25.352	
Fisher J M	Capt RM	27.264	
Fitzgerald	Mr	4.168	at Totnes
Fitzgerald	Capt RN	4.256	at Weymouth
Flahau	Lt Count	38.87	at Edinburgh
Flamank	Miss	31.87	of Newton Abbott
Fleetwood	Lt	7.452	
Fleming Archibald	Mr	20.256	
Fletcher Henry		24.85	at Malta
Fletcher James		25.174	
		25.352	
Flint John Campbell	MD	20.80	
Flower	Miss	24.174	
Foley Emily Jane	Miss	25.439	
		26.87	
Foote William	Capt RN	3.156	
Foote Edward James	Capt RN	10.175	
		10.263	
Forbes	Lt RN	8.87	of Plymouth
Forbes John	Capt RN	32.176	
Ford	Miss	23.350	at Portlock
Ford R M	RN	26.515	
Ford	Miss	27.264	at Calcutta
Ford	Lt RN	31.87	at Plymouth
Fordyce Barbara	Miss	23.175	
Fordyce Charlotte	Miss	31.352	
Forster Charlotte	Miss	7.532	
Forster A C		14.262	
Forster	Miss	25.86	of Liverpool
Forster	Capt RN	26.264	at Plymton
Foster George		28.513	
Foster Maria	Miss	34.439	
Fostier Augustus W		8.439	
Fowler R Merrick	Capt RN	29.511	
Fox	Miss	1.347	
Foy Robert	Capt RM	26.351	
Fracey F	Miss	34.352	
Francklyn	Miss	11.343	of Bath
Frank Frank	R Adm	30.447	
Frankland Henry A		25.86	ex 23rd Dragoon Guards
Franklin	Lt RN	8.520	

Franklin J R	Capt HEIC	19.86	
Franklyn James		33.87	
Franks Margaret	Miss	13.335	
Fraser Sarah A	Miss	3.420	
		3.516	
Fraser	Lt RN	16.264	
Fraser Lillias	Miss	25.263	
Freeman Stella F	Mrs	2.171	
Freeth Harriett	Miss	40.164	
French	Miss	14.511	late of Loughrea, Ireland, at Plymouth
Fricker	Lt RN	10.350	
Frodsham	Miss	23.519	
Fuller	Lt RN	23.440	at Gibraltar
Fyers	Miss	7.532	at Gibraltar
		8.87	
Gage Charlotte	Miss	7.452	
Galbraith Archibald		4.347	
Galbraith Catharine	Miss	4.347	
Gambier Mary	Miss	30.175	
		30.359	
Gambier R	Capt RN	34.440	
Gamble Robert		27.86	
Gardiner T	Lt RN	27.438	
Gardiner Charles		28.439	
Gardner H	Capt Hon	12.431	
Gardner	R Adm, Rt Hon Lord	21.352	
Gardner John		24.85	
Gardner Val. Wm	Capt RN, Hon	24.175	
Gascoyne John	Capt RN	2.448	
Gascoyne	Lt Col HEIC	20.493	at St George's Hanover Square
Gay William		25.86	
Geddes John	Lt RN	28.439	
George James	Capt	6.348	
George Sarah	Miss	25.86	at St Peter's, Dublin
Gerrard William	Capt RN	25.86	at Belfast
Gibbs Mary	Miss	24.438	
Gibson	Miss	16.175	at St Lawrence, Isle of Thanet
Gibson Thos		27.438	
Gibson Dorothy	Miss	38.88	
Giddy Charles	Capt RN	38.176	
Giffard John	Capt RN	8.439	
Gifford James	Reverend	19.515	
Gilbank William	Reverend	33.87	
Gilbert	Capt	24.351	at Falmouth
Gill Richard	Capt	24.351	
Gill Mary	Miss	25.86	
Gill E T	Lt RN	27.438	
Gill George	Lt RM	28.513	
Gillmore Mary	Miss	14.511	
Gittens	Mr	30.359	at Portsmouth
Glanvill	Lt RN	22.88	
Glanville	Miss	5.280	of Plymouth
Glasse C	Mrs	25.352	

Glegram	Miss	18.174	of Plymouth Dock
Glode	Miss	33.351	of Aske Terrace, City Road
Gloucester	Duke of	36.86	
Glynn H R	Capt	11.493	
Gobbett	Miss	2.547	the bride given away by Lord Nelson
Goble Barbara	Miss	29.263	
Godbold Susanna E	Miss	35.440	
Godden	Miss	9.497	of Portsea
Godfrey	Lt HEIC	20.80	
Godfrey Thomas		30.521	Halifax, Nova Scotia
Godfrey P	Lt RN	38.88	
Gold	Miss	31.175	of Gillingham
Goldie Emily	Mrs	19.352	
Golightly	Miss	4.168	
Golding Hannah M	Miss	27.86	
Goldsmith H C	Lt RN	32.439	
		33.87	
Goldson William		25.263	
Gooch	Mr	26.178	of Haslar Hospital
Goodwin Eleanor	Miss	27.175	
Gordon Elizabeth	Mrs	10.175	
Gordon	Miss	21.264	at Marylebone Church
Gordon J M	Capt RN	25.85	
Gordon J A	Capt	28.263	
Gore	Miss	9.423	at East Horsley
Gore Ralph	Lt RN	19.439	at Cloyne
Gore John	Capt RN, Sir	20.167	by special licence
Gosselin T Le M	Capt RN	21.264	
Gould D	Capt RN	9.497	
Gould	Mr	14.262	at Honiton
Gould Eliza	Miss	32.438	
Graham	Miss	5.187	of Hatton Garden
Graham E	Miss	15.264	
Graham Thomas	Capt RN	24.86	at Bombay
Graham Sarah	Miss	28.438	
Grant Grace	Miss	22.352	
Grant Thomas		26.264	
Grant James Charles		30.359	
Grant Walter Edward		33.351	
Gravenor Mary	Miss	28.513	
Graves Margaret	the Hon	8.439	
Graves C	Miss	31.87	of St John's Newfoundland
Graves Anna	Miss	33.176	
Gray Jane	Miss	4.347	
Gray S	Miss	13.164	
Gray Francis E		23.87	
Graydon	Miss	15.87	
Greaves Thomas	V Adm Sir	20.166	
Greaves	Lt RN	32.351	
Green Joshua		25.263	
Greenlaw	Capt RN	32.263	
Greenly Elizabeth	Miss	25.352	
Greenly Isaac C	V Adm Sir	25.352	known formerly as Sir Isaac Coffin
Greensill	Capt RN	27.264	

Name	Title	Ref	Notes
Greentree J		27.438	
Greenway Samuel	Lt RN	24.515	
Greenwood Ann	Miss	32.511	
Greetham	Miss	25.513	of E. Cosham, at Widley, Hants
Gregory Anne	Miss	27.438	
Greig Samuel	Capt	12.86	of the Imperial Russian Navy
Grenfel Fanny	Miss	23.519	
Gretham Frances	Miss	30.87	
Grey Hannah	Lady	18.347	
Grey G	Lt RN	34.351	
Griffiths A J	Capt RN	7.532	
Griffiths	Miss	3.156	
Grindall Ann	Miss	26.263	
Gritten	Lt RM	29.263	at Woolwich
Groube	Capt RN	24.174	at Madras
Grove	Lt RN	9.165	
Grover J	Reverend	26.264	
Gullett John		23.264	at Halifax, Nova Scotia
Gumbleton	Miss	7.452	of County Waterford, at Bath
Gunn	Miss	34.440	of Mount Kennedy, Ireland, at Newcastle
Gunney	Miss	7.532	
Guy R E		26.515	
Guyon G H	Lt RM	1.540	
Guyon	Lt	11.493	
Gwern	Capt	32.263	of the Royal Hussars
Hadley John		18.519	
Hadsley	Miss	21.264	of Ware Priory, Herts
Hales Mary	Miss	33.87	
Hall	Miss	9.81	at Old Windsor Church
Hall	Lt RN	18.519	at Bamburgh
Hall Eliza	Miss	19.439	
Hall Caroline	Miss	26.264	
Hall Theophila	Miss	29.174	
Hall Robert	Capt RM	34.511	
Hall W	Capt RN	35.263	
Hallam Lydia	Miss	32.351	
Hallett Anne	Miss	29.511	
Halliday J		32.263	
Halliday Elizabeth	Miss	38.176	
Hallowell B	Capt RN	3.331	
Halsey Emilia	Miss	24.262	
Halstead	Capt RN	10.350	
Hambly N	Miss	26.514	at Gibraltar
Hamilton Charles	RN, Sir	9.339	by special licence
Hamilton Edward	Capt RN, Sir	12.431	by special licence at St George's Hanover Sq.
Hamilton Augustus		13.335	
Hamilton	Viscount	22.520	by special licence
Hammersley Diana	Miss	29.263	
Hammick Eliz. Love	Miss	26.514	
Hammond Francis T	Col	10.87	
Hammond	Miss	12.341	
Hammond	Miss	12.86	of Hull
Hammond	Miss	23.350	of Northwold, Norfolk

Name	Title	Ref	Note
Hanchett	Miss	25.85	
Hancock	Capt RN	26.515	at Bath
Hancock R T	Capt RN	29.87	
Hanmer	Miss	28.262	of Holbrook Hall, Suffolk
Hanwell William	Capt RN	3.420	
Hanwell	Miss	3.420	
Harding James		28.87	
Harding	Miss	33.351	of Portsea
Hardinge George N	Capt	20.483	
Hardy Temple	Capt RN	4.526	
Hardy	Miss	11.493	
Hardy Thomas M	Capt Sir	19.86	at Halifax
Hardy	Miss	29.87	of Plymouth
Hardyman L F	Capt RN	25.86	
Hardyman William H		25.263	
Hare Mary	Miss	3.420	
Hargood William	R Adm	25.439	
Harley	Miss	12.86	
Harmood	Miss	12.86	
Harness	Doctor	31.352	
Harral	Mr	27.175	at Ipswich
Harris	Miss	12.431	at Bersted near Havant
Harris	Capt RN	14.350	at St George's, Hanover Sq.
Harris T H		24.86	of HEIC, at Bengal
Harris Susan	Miss	26.178	
Harris George	Lt RN	33.351	
Harrison Jane	Miss	25.86	
Harrison Charles R		27.351	
Harrison	Miss	32.351	at Cheltenham
Harston S R		19.352	
Hart R	Miss	23.264	at Halifax, Nova Scotia
Hartshorne	Miss	33.87	of Halifax, Nova Scotia
Hartley	Mr	5.96	Master of the Arrow
Harvey	Miss	12.341	by special licence at St George's, Hanover Sq.
Harvey Thomas	Capt	13.335	
Harvey Sarah	Miss	13.335	
Hartwell Francis	Sir	27.264	by special licence
Harvey Elizabeth	Miss	26.438	
Harvey Georgiana	Miss	35.352	
Harvey Elizabeth	Miss	35.440	
Harwood	Capt RN	23.87	at Charles near Plymouth
Hassall Esther	Miss	27.438	
Hastings Francis	Lt	4.444	
Haswell	Miss	25.85	of Plymouth Dock
Haultain	Miss	1.174	
Haultain Charles	Capt RN	32.263	
Hawford Sophia	Miss	29.87	
Hawker Dorothea	Miss	4.168	
Hawker	Miss	7.180	
Hawker	Miss	11.87	at Plymouth
Hawker	Miss	30.87	of Woolwich Yard
Hawker	Miss	33.87	daughter of Edward Hawker
Hawker	Miss	33.511	daughter of Rev Dr D Hawker
Hawkey C	Capt RN	31.438	at Madras
Hawkins G D	Lt RM	24.262	

Hawkins Jane	Miss	30.522	
Hawtayne	Capt RN	19.439	
Hay	Miss	19.439	at Cloyne
Hay Catharine	Miss	25.263	
Haydon Nathaniel		26.514	
Haydon Samuel		29.87	
Hayles Jane	Miss	10.438	
Hayley	Lt RN	29.439	
Haynes P	Miss	13.423	
Haynes George		14.174	
Haynes Sophia	Miss	27.351	
Haynes L	Miss	27.514	
Haynes Henry	Capt RN	35.86	
Hayter Mary	Miss	17.520	
Hearsey	Miss	22.88	of Denmark Hill, Surrey
			at Brixham, Devon
Heath Rose	Miss	29.87	at Fahn, near Derry
Hellard J	Lt RN	12.431	
Hellard	Miss	34.440	of Plymouth
Hembry John		29.352	at Cronstadt, Russia
Hemphill S		15.440	
Henry	Miss	1.347	
Hepburn G S	Lt HEIC	20.80	
Hervey	Miss	31.352	of Torpoint
Hetherington	Mrs	11.493	at Blackfriars
Hewson	Capt RN	19.352	
Heylon	Miss	32.262	of Lymington, Hants
Heylyn	Mrs	3.240	
Heynes Ann	Miss	35.175	
Heywood Edmund	Capt RN	33.176	
Hibberd Martha	Miss	12.165	
Hichins Cuthbert	Capt	32.263	
Hicks	Miss	14.350	of Enbourne
Hicks P W H		22.88	
Hicks George		29.263	
Hicks Charlotte A	Miss	34.440	at Jersey
Hicks Sarah	Miss	34.440	
Higgins	Capt RN	35.175	at Kingston Church
Hill	Miss	3.156	
Hill	Capt RN	13.85	
Hill	Mrs	17.439	of Plymouth Dock
Hill Eliza	Miss	20.255	
Hill William	Capt RN	23.439	
Hill (i)	Miss	27.514	at Antigua
Hill (ii)	Miss	27.514	at Antigua
Hill	Capt RN	32.87	
Hills William	Capt RN	6.516	
Hills George	Capt RN	29.263	
Hills	Lt RN	33.176	at Stoke Church
Hillyar James	Capt RN	14.262	in Malta
Hillyar	Miss	27.351	at Plymouth
Hillyar Robert P		31.175	
Hilton George	Capt RN	35.440	
Hire George A		23.440	
Hoam Chi Altaugi	Miss	27.175	at Canton, China
Hobson Emma	Miss	33.87	

Hocart	Miss	19.176	of Weymouth
Hodder	Capt RN	9.165	
Hodge	Miss	26.350	
Hodges Elizabeth	Miss	32.351	
Hoeken Augusta	Miss	32.87	
Holden	Miss	9.251	of Yarmouth
Hole Francis	Capt RM	26.178	
Hole Lewis	Capt RN	36.86	
Hollingworth	Capt RN	21.87	
Holloway	Miss	6.172	daughter of R Adm Holloway
Holloway Emily	Miss	18.267	of Emsworth, at Warblington
Holmes Maria	Miss	2.171	
Holmes	Capt RM	12.86	
Holmes William	Lt RN	32.438	
Holroyd Mary Ann	Miss	24.514	
Hood	Capt	12.341	son of the Hon Col Hood
Hood	Commodore	13.85	at Barbadoes
Hood	the Hon, Miss	14.86	
Hood Samuel	Hon	24.85	
Hood Alexander	Sir	34.176	
Hope Robert		4.444	aged 80 yrs, to a girl of 13
Hope G	Capt RN	9.165	
Hopkins	Miss	30.175	of Newton Abbott
Hopkins	Lt RN	32.351	
Hopkins F		35.516	
Hore Charity E	Miss	32.439	
		33.87	
Hornby Phipps	Capt RN	33.87	
Hornsby	Miss	16.264	at Kingston, near Portsmouth
Horton Joshua S		19.86	
Hotchkis John	Lt	4.444	
Hotham William	Capt RN	11.493	
Hotham	Miss	13.164	
Hough John James	Lt RN	34.352	
How	Miss	23.175	of Chatham
Howard	Miss	23.519	at Bermuda
Howatson John		26.178	
Howe	Baroness	28.438	widow of the Hon Penn Ashton Curzon
Howell	Miss	32.511	at Bath
Hoy	Miss	18.174	
Hudson	Mrs	26.350	
Hughes Charles		20.167	at Cape of Good Hope
Hulbert G H		27.514	
Humphrey William O		30.359	
Humphreys	Capt RN	13.245	
Humphreys	Capt RN	23.519	
Hunt William	Lt RM	27.175	
Hunter Hannah	Mrs	7.180	
Hurst S F	Miss	16.88	
Husband Mary	Miss	24.351	
Huskisson William	MP	1.446	
Hutcheson Mary	Miss	20.80	
Hutcheson	Lt RN	34.439	at Bath
Hutchinson	Doctor	14.511	
Hutchison Catherine	Miss	33.440	at Bermuda

Hutton Andrew	Capt	24.263	
Hyde	Miss	13.335	
Hyde J C		33.176	
		33.351	
Hyndman	Miss	28.439	at Uplyme
Impey J	Capt RN	20.423	married at Gretna Green
Inches J		28.262	
Inglefield	Miss	3.331	
Inglis Jane	Miss	35.440	at Amhendening
Ingram	Lt RN	16.264	
Ingram	Adm	26.263	
Ingram G		30.521	
Irby	Capt RN	10.517	
Ireland J	Lt RN	11.421	
Isbell E	Miss	26.351	
Ives	Miss	15.351	at Bungay
Ivie	Lt RN	18.347	at St Hillier's, Jersey
Jackson	Miss	21.87	of Plymouth
Jackson Rebecca	Miss	26.178	at Calcutta
		26.350	
Jackson	Capt	27.351	at Gosport
Jackson Robert M	Capt RN	32.351	
Jacob	Miss	22.88	at Deal
Jacques	Lt RN	12.431	
Jaffray J Richmond		29.511	
Jager Elizabeth	Miss	30.447	
Jago F J		21.519	
Jagoe	Miss	25.174	
James Henrietta	Miss	19.351	
James Harriet	Miss	23.440	
Jane Henry	Capt RN	28.439	
Jarvoise	Miss	27.438	of Kingston
Jeans	Lt RN	24.351	
Jebson Ann	Miss	34.440	
Jeffreys	Miss	14.262	of Portsea
Jeffreys	Miss	25.439	of Swansea, at Tremington, Devon
Jeffries	Miss	26.87	of Fratton
Jekyll John		1.261	
Jenison E M	Miss	28.352	
Jenkins	Miss	8.87	of Plymouth
Jenkins William	Lt	23.439	
Jenkins Maria	Miss	25.263	
Jenkinson	Miss	15.264	of Portsmouth
Jenkinson Anne M	Miss	23.439	
Jenney Agnes	Miss	26.350	
Jennings	Mr	6.84	of the Maidstone
Jesson Sarah	Miss	33.87	
Jessop	Mr	28.87	Purser RN
Jeynes	Miss	8.520	of Gloucester
Jeynes	Miss	11.493	
Jeynes Mary	Miss	28.87	of Cork
Jiff Thomas	Lt RN	29.263	
Johns	Mr	24.438	

Johns Mary	Miss	25.513	
Johns S	Lt RN	30.87	
Johnson William		3.156	
Johnson Anne G H	Miss	24.85	
Johnson P		25.174	
Johnstone Charlotte	Miss	4.256	
Johnstone	Lady	9.165	
Johnstone William	Capt RM	22.264	
Johnstone Sarah	Miss	22.520	
Johnstone Cochrane	Miss	35.352	
Johnstone Frederick		38.176	
Jones	Miss	5.187	dau of Mr J of the Exchequer
Jones David		7.532	
Jones	Mrs	14.350	at Weymouth
Jones T	Reverend	18.83	
Jones	Capt Hon	18.267	
Jones William	Capt	19.515	
Jones	Capt	24.515	at Woolwich
Jones J E	Lt RM	27.438	
Jones Frances	Miss	34.511	
Jones J		34.512	at Gosport
Jukes	Miss	16.264	of Gosport
Julian J T K	Lt RN	25.85	
Kains	Capt RN	31.175	
Kane Patrick		15.264	
Katon	Capt RN	11.263	
Katon Maria J	Miss	27.514	
Kearney	Miss	18.174	at Edinburgh
		18.267	
Keast	Miss	26.351	at St Germain's
Keats Rebecca	Miss	33.511	
Keen	Miss	34.439	
Keenor	Lt RN	2.448	
Keir W G	Sir	26.178	at Calcutta
		26.350	
Keith	Lord	19.86	by special licence
Keith Mouat	Miss	37.85	at Calcutta
Kellett	Capt RM	6.516	
Kelly M M		30.264	
Kelynash	Miss	24.351	at Paul Church near Penzance
Kemp R		8.439	shipwright employed at Constantinople
Kempster W H		30.87	
Kempthorne Ellen	Miss	31.438	
Kennedy John		24.514	
Kent Sarah T	Miss	16.514	
Kent Eliza	Miss	30.359	
Kent Euphemia	Miss	34.439	
Kent Robena	Miss	35.86	
Kentish	Miss	25.263	of Weovil nr Gosport
Kentish Samuel	Lt RN	31.175	
Kernan	Lt RN	30.522	
Kerr Alexander R	Lt	4.444	
Kerr	Capt RN	13.85	
Kerr Mary	Miss	27.175	

Kew	Miss	29.174	at St Margaret's, Westminster
Key W S	Lt RN	16.88	
Kilvington Orfeur W	Reverend	36.174	
King A	Miss	7.92	
King	Miss	10.87	
King R	Capt RN	10.517	
King	Miss	12.431	of Penrith
King	Miss	15.176	of Titchfield
King Maria	Miss	27.175	
King George	Lt RN	27.438	
King Mary Ann	Miss	29.174	
King Edward	Capt RN	33.511	
King	Capt RN, Hon	34.511	
Kingsman	Miss	29.263	
Kinneer	Miss	29.87	at Salisbury
Kirby	Miss	19.86	of Marlborough
Kirby Walter	Lt RN	33.87	
Kirk Anne	Miss	24.174	
Kirkland	Miss	19.439	at Bath
Kirkpatrick	Miss	18.347	at Marylebone Church
Kitson R		14.511	
Kitson R R		25.263	
Kittoe	Miss	20.335	
Knight	Miss	4.526	
Knight Joseph		5.375	
Knight	Lt RN	7.92	
Knight	Mrs	20.335	at Kingston Church
Knight Susan	Miss	33.511	
Knighton William	Doctor	4.168	
Knowle Edward		38.88	
Knowles Charles H	R Adm Sir	4.256	
Knox	Miss	5.375	at Edinburgh
Lackington G		13.246	
Lacon Ann	Miss	31.87	
Lacy T de	Reverend	16.88	
Laffer P		28.176	
Laird Mary	Miss	11.263	
Laird William B		19.439	
Lake John	Lt RN	5.280	
Lake Sophia	Miss	23.87	
Lambert John	Lt RN	23.175	p.o.w. at Verdun
Lambert Henry	Capt	26.264	
Lambert Henry	Mrs	32.263	
Lane	Mr	27.264	
Lane	Lt RM	29.511	at Woolwich
Langborne Nathaniel		20.335	
Langford Lucinda	Miss	1.540	
Langford	Capt RN	9.497	
Langham S	Miss	4.444	
Langley S	Lt RN	33.511	
Lapidge	Lt RN	38.87	
Laprimandaye Louisa	Miss	28.352	
Lark Henry		28.513	
Larkan A	Miss	20.256	
Larke William		21.87	

Latham T H	Capt RM	2.644	
Laudell W		18.267	
Laugherne	Miss	15.87	at Alverstoke
Lawford	Capt RN	9.251	
Lawlor Sophia	Miss	19.86	
Lawrence Lucy	Miss	2.263	
Lawrence Louisa	Miss	27.438	
Lawrence	Miss	31.175	of Plymouth Dock
Lawry	Mrs	28.176	
Lawson James		26.350	
Lawson G		27.514	
Lawson Ann Lindsay	Miss	30.264	
Lea	Miss	1.540	
Leake	Miss	8.520	
Leaman William		26.86	
Leave Sarah	Miss	25.513	
Lechmere Mary	Miss	32.351	
Lee John Theophilus		19.86	
Lee	Miss	29.352	at Honiton
L'Egere	Miss	23.440	at Gibraltar
Le Geyt	Capt RN	29.87	at Fahn near Derry
Legrand Susannah	Miss	34.440	at Cork
Le Grice	Miss	16.264	at Stonehouse
Le Gros	Capt RN	12.511	at Jersey
Leigh	Miss	23.175	p.o.w. at Verdun
Le Mesurier	Miss	12.511	at Guernsey
Lemon	Mrs	31.175	of Plymouth Dockyard
Lemon	Mr	31.175	Purser RN
Lemorie	Mrs	12.511	at Jersey
Leroux	Lt	19.86	
Leslie Walter	Lt RN	38.88	
Lewis E		23.519	
Lewis James		28.352	
Ley T H	Reverend	27.351	
Lillicrap	Capt RN	27.86	
Lidden Ann	Miss	28.263	
Linthorne	Capt RN	33.511	
Lintott W H		20.335	
Linzee	Mrs	31.352	
Lipson	Lt RN	28.176	at Weymouth
Little	Mr, junior	27.86	
Little Mary	Miss	28.352	
Little	Miss	28.513	of Camberwell
Little James		31.438	
Little	Mr	33.511	of Portsmouth Dockyard
Littlehales	Capt RN	10.263	
Littlejohn Isabella	Miss	26.178	
Littleton Hugh	Reverend	32.351	
Lloyd	Miss	4.527	
Lloyd	Miss	10.87	of Rhosbeirio
Lloyd William		12.341	by special licence
Lloyd D	Reverend	19.352	
Lloyd	Miss	19.439	
Lloyd Dorinda	Miss	24.352	
Lloyd John Burnaby		26.264	
Lock John		23.350	

Lock	Miss	33.511	of Norbury Park
Locker	Doctor	21.352	
Lockyer	Miss	7.452	
Lockyer Edmund H		33.351	
Lockwood H	Miss	9.251	
Loney de	Miss	34.352	
Long Edward Lawson		18.174	
Long Walter	R Adm	23.175	by special licence
Long	Mrs	26.86	at Sunning-hill, Berks
Long	Miss	29.174	of Portsmouth
Longuet Elizabeth	Miss	26.515	
Lord J J		26.351	
Loring John W	Capt RN	12.86	
		12.255	
Loring Mary	Mrs	24.352	
Losack Woodley	Capt RN	21.264	
Louis John	Capt RN, Sir	18.347	
Louis Anne-Eleanor	Miss	27.351	
Louis Jane-Frances	Miss	27.351	
Loveless Elizabeth	Miss	7.180	
Lovell	Lt RN	7.452	
Lowcay William	Lt RN	31.175	
Lowcey	Lt	10.87	
Lowe A	Lt RN	7.532	
Lowry	Miss	17.263	at Chatham
Lowry Robert W		33.176	
Lowther C B P	Reverend	12.341	
Lucas James	Lt RN	4.444	
Lucas M	Miss	16.352	
Luce John	Capt RN	1.261	
Lucinde	Miss	33.264	at Fareham
Luckey D	Capt RN	13.245	
Luckcraft William	Lt	33.511	
Luddington Joseph	Lt RN	38.88	
Lugger	Miss	27.86	of Plymouth Dock
Lumley	Capt RN	26.264	at Hamble, Hants
Lumsden John		26.178	
Luscombe M H	Reverend	12.86	
Lyford Henry	Capt RN	29.263	
Lyne Philip	Lt RN	4.347	
Lyne Sarah	Miss	32.351	
Lynne Thomas		4.167	
Lyons Edmund	Capt RN	32.176	
		32.262	
Lys James Oades	Lt RN	27.264	
Lysaght Arthur	Capt RN	29.263	
MacArthur T		18.174	
M'Arthur H H		27.175	
M'Carthy Honora	Miss	20.423	
M'Comb James		27.175	at Canton, China
M'Coy	Miss	8.439	
M'Coy Alexander		21.176	
MacCulloch W	Capt RN	24.514	
M'Curdy	Miss	18.267	at St John's, Newfoundland
M'Donald William		4.526	

M'Dougall Sarah	Miss	9.165	m. Lt Wyborn, 18th Drag.
M'Dougall	Miss	9.165	m. Lt Masson RA
M'Dougall	Adm	16.175	
M'Dougall	Miss	18.437	of Catton
M'Dougall Jane	Miss	26.87	
Mac-Ewan Rachel	Miss	26.178	
M'Farlane James		23.519	
M'Gie	Miss	18.347	in Newfoundland
McGory	Miss	28.438	at Halifax
M'Inherney W		34.352	
M'Kay E B	Miss	4.526	
MacKay William	MD	25.440	
MacKay Margaret C	Miss	34.439	
MacIntosh Jessy	Miss	26.350	
M'Kenzie	Miss	13.85	at Barbadoes
M'Kenzie Mary	Miss	23.519	
MacKey	Lt RM	20.255	
MacKie	Mrs	18.267	
M'Killip	Miss	6.172	
MacKintosh Cath	Miss	28.438	at Bagdaad
M'Laughlin B		29.87	
M'Lean	Miss	38.88	at Halifax, Nova Scotia
MacNamara	Miss	12.431	by special licence, at St George's, Hanover Square
MacNamara	Miss	18.347	at St Christopher's
Maddock	Miss	16.88	of Portsmouth
Maddock Eleanor	Miss	24.351	
Madore Mary	Miss	22.88	
Mainwaring Rowland		25.85	
Mainwaring	Capt	38.176	of the 10th Foot, Malta
Malcolm Charles	Capt RN	19.515	
Malcolm P	Capt RN	21.87	
Maling	Capt RN	26.515	at Breadsall
Mallack	Miss	11.421	
Mallough Sophia M	Miss	26.515	
Mallet Louisa	Miss	26.178	
Malone C	Miss	27.175	
Manby Thomas	Capt RN	23.350	
Mangles George	Reverend	24.174	
Manley Wm		12.165	
Manley	Miss	14.262	at Croydon
Manley	Miss	23.519	at Plymouth
Mann Amelia	Miss	18.347	
Mann C	Reverend	18.437	
Mannorch	Lt Col	14.262	
Mansell	Capt RN	13.504	
Mansell H L	Reverend	34.176	
Mant Thomas		30.175	
		30.359	
Mantle Octavia	Miss	33.87	
Manwaring William		19.352	
Maples J F	Capt RN	31.438	
March Augusta M	Miss	38.88	
Marchant Thomas		24.174	
Markett	Lt RN	14.262	at Croydon
Markland J D	Capt RN	31.262	

Marley	R R	Lt RN	28.262	
Marsh		Mr	30.175	
			30.359	
Marshall	Rebecca M	Miss	11.87	
Marshall		Miss	19.352	
Marshall		Miss	28.87	of Hardway nr Gosport
Marshall	Eliza A	Miss	28.262	
Marshall	S	Lt RN	29.174	
Marshall	Elizabeth	Miss	31.511	
Marshall	Elizabeth	Miss	32.351	
Marshall	M	Miss	32.351	
Marshall	Jane	Miss	34.352	
Marshall	Nanny	Miss	34.440	
Martin	G	Capt RN	11.343	
Martin		Capt RN	24.515	
Martin	John		27.86	
Martin	John		27.175	
Martin	J P	Lt RN	30.87	
Martin	George	V Adm Sir	33.511	
Martyr	Charles		38.88	at Halifax, Nova Scotia
Mary		HRH Princess	36.86	
Masefield		Capt RN	8.520	
Mason	Francis	Capt RN	14.86	
Mason		Mr	25.174	at Stoke Ch, Plymouth
Massey	G	Reverend	23.519	
Masson	Thomas	Lt RA	9.165	
Mathews	W T J	Capt RM	24.174	
			24.352	
Mathews	R B	Lt RN	30.447	
Matson		Capt RN	32.351	at Cheltenham
Matthews	Mary	Miss	24.438	
Maude		Capt RN	29.511	at St Martin's in the Fields
Maude	Maria	Miss	33.176	
			33.351	
Maughan	J	of HEIC	18.174	
Maughan	J	Capt RM	23.440	
Maule	C	Miss	13.85	
Maund	H	Miss	26.350	
Maund	John		27.514	
Maurice	F M	Lt RN	11.175	
Maurice	J W	Capt RN	32.351	
Maxwell	Eleanora L	Miss	24.351	
Maxwell	Hester	Miss	30.359	
May		Capt RN	31.87	
Mayhew		Miss	22.175	at Stoke Church
Mayne		Lt RN	14.511	at Gibraltar
Mayton		Miss	28.176	of Faversham at Portsmouth
Meade		Miss	9.339	
Mearns	R A	Miss	24.85	
Mends	Robert	Capt RN	8.352	
Menzies	Charlotte	Lady	5.464	
Mercer	Elphinstone	the Hon Miss	38.87	at Edinburgh
Meredith		Lt RM	14.350	
Metcalfe		Miss	28.176	at Mary le bone Church
Methuen	Gertrude G	Miss	33.351	
Meurer	Cornelia J		26.439	re-married Wm. Jas. Mingay

Middleton	Capt RN	8.520	
Milbanke	Miss	1.446	
Millard J		20.80	
Miller	Lt	23.519	at Bermuda
Miller Ann	Miss	25.439	
Miller Eleanor	Miss	33.351	
Mills	Miss	30.175	of Portsea
		30.359	
Milne D	Capt RN	11.421	
Milne Sarah	Miss	25.86	at Belfast
Minet Isaac		8.176	
Mingay William J		26.439	re-married Cornelia Johannah Meurer
Minnis Sophia Ann	Miss	30.521	at Halifax, Nova Scotia
Minto	Major RMA	28.513	
Mitchell	Miss	8.352	of Gosport at Alverstoke
Mitchell Louisa	Miss	14.350	
Mitchell	Capt RA	15.87	
Mitchell	Miss	24.515	of Portsea
Mitchell Susan	Miss	25.86	
Mitchell	Miss	27.175	
Mitchell Spalding	Lt RN	38.87/88	
Mitford	Mrs	21.351	nee Anstruther
Moffat William	Capt HEIC	27.86	
Moffat	Lt RN	29.174	
Moir Anthony R L		26.515	
Molland Ann	Miss	26.350	
Molloy	Miss	21.519	by special licence
Moncrief J		20.80	
Moncrieff Isabella	Miss	10.175	
Moncrieff James		19.515	
Money Maria	Miss	14.350	
Money Rowland	Lt RN	14.350	
Money Sarah	Miss	27.86	
Monk E A	Miss	13.245	
Monkton	Capt RN	18.267	
Monro James		13.335	
Montagu	Miss	20.167	by special licence
Moor Francis	Colonel	7.276	
Moore	Capt RN	18.267	of Emsworth at Warblington
Moore William		24.263	
Moore Graham	Capt RN	27.264	by special licence
Moorson Margaret	Miss	34.176	
Moran	Miss	26.515	of Portsea
Moresby Fairfax	Capt RN	32.263	
Morgan Maria	Miss	20.493	
Morgan Ann	Miss	26.350	
Morgan John F	Capt RN	34.440	
Moriarty Martha	Miss	34.439	
Moriarty J R	Lt RM	34.440	
Morier J P		32.511	
Morin T	Miss	13.245	
Morley	Miss	7.452	
Morris James Nicol	Capt RN	8.439	
Morris	Lt RN	13.423	
Morris	Capt RN	18.437	at Minster, Sheppy

Morris or Morres Ed	Lt RN	20.80	by special licence
		20.167	disavowal of previous entry
Morris S		24.514	
Morritt Edward		6.84	
Morsley Richard	Capt RN	5.280	
Mortimer	Miss	18.267	
Morton	Mr	34.176	of HMS Alban
Moser	Miss	9.165	of Chepstow
Moss William		25.513	
Mottley	Mr	17.520	of the Customs
Mouat	Miss	33.351	at Calcutta
Moubray R H	Capt RN	33.87	
Mould T	Lt RM	11.493	
Mould John	Capt RN	34.351	
Moultrie Cecilia	Miss	22.176	
Mounier	Lt RN	23.350	at Kinsale
Mounsher	Capt RN	24.438	
Moutray	Miss	16.88	
Mowbray	Mrs	9.423	
Mowbray	Miss	11.263	of Gosport
Moxon	Lt RN	30.359	at Halifax
Moyer Thomas		27.264	
Muddle Richard H		22.176	at St John's, Newfoundland
Mugford	Mr	24.515	
Mulcaster Howe	Capt RN	32.351	
Mules	Lt RN	9.339	
Murray	Miss	11.87	
Murray	Miss	24.85	at Mary-le-bone
Muston T G	Capt RN	35.440	
Nagle Luke F	Doctor	32.439	
Napier Charles	Capt RN	34.88	
Napier W J	Capt RN	35.352	
Napier	the Hon, Miss	36.174	
Nash	Miss	22.352	at Anthony, Tor Point
Nash John	Capt RN	24.352	
Nash M S	Miss	32.351	
Neave	Capt RN	7.532	
Needham Selina	Miss	38.88	
Nelson G		4.526	
Nelson Charlotte	Lady	24.85	Nelson's niece
Nepean John	Lt RN	18.347	
Nepean C W		39.343	
Nesbitt	Capt RN	25.352	
Nesbitt Wm		28.176	
Nesham	Capt RN	8.439	
Ness Eliza Cecilia	Miss	24.438	
Neville	Lord Viscount	29.174	
Nevillie H W	Reverend	18.347	
New	Capt	10.438	
Newcombe F	Capt RN	27.175	
Newcombe Jane	Miss	30.359	
Newnham George L		35.516	
Newman	Lt	19.176	
Nicholson James	Capt	19.86	
Nicholson	Miss	26.350	of Portsea Island

Nicholson Eliza	Miss	33.87	
Nightingale David T	Lt RN	33.351	
Noble	Miss	18.519	of Bellford
Noddie	Mrs	34.512	of Gosport
Noel Augusta Julia	the Hon	32.176	
Noel	Capt Hon	34.352	at Bloxworth, Devon
Norbury Phillippa	Miss	14.174	
Norman	Miss	14.86	
North	Miss	7.532	of Portsea
Norton George	Lt RN	3.331	
Nosworthy Eliza P	Miss	30.87	
Oake Josiah		25.513	
Oakeley	Miss	27.264	of Monmouth
Oates	Miss	18.347	of Bellair nr Falmouth
Obrien James	Capt RN	4.526	
O'Brien E	R Adm	19.352	
O'Brien Ann	Miss	27.438	at Cork
O'Brien C	Capt RN	34.439	
O'Bryen E	Capt RN	13.164	
O'Bryen Edward	Capt RN, Lord	33.351	
O'Connel	Lt Col	24.438	at Sydney, N.S.W.
Odell John W	Lt RN	5.375	
Odell G		16.264	
Ogilvy	Capt RN	7.452	
Ogle C	Capt RN	7.452	
Okeley	Miss	24.85	at Radipool
Oldfield T B		29.174	
Oliver James		6.84	
Oliver R D	Capt RN	14.86	by special licence
Ollesson(i)	Miss	13.245	
Ollesson(ii)	Miss	13.245	
Omer H M	Miss	6.84	
Ommanney H M	Capt RN	11.263	
Ommanney Ann	Miss	33.351	
Onion	Miss	25.263	of Priddy's Yard, near Gosport
Onslow	Miss	4.526	43 yrs younger than her groom
Onslow M R		14.511	
O'Reilly Edward	Capt	15.87	Warwickshire Militia
O'Reilly	Capt RN	34.352	at Truro
Orkney	Lt RN	24.85	at Barking Church
Orrock	Miss	29.352	
Osborn Jane B	Miss	24.514	
Osborne	Capt RN	11.87	
Otter	Capt RN	16.175	
Otway Robert W	Capt RN	6.172	
Outram Benjamin		25.439	
Ovey Mabella Ann	Miss	28.262	
Owen E W C R	Capt RN	9.165	
Padurck William Jnr.	Mr	30.447	
Page	Mr	20.335	
Paget C	Hon	13.245	
Paisley	Miss	4.168	
Palk R		17.439	
Palmer D	Miss	9.497	

Palmer	C	Miss	15.440	
Palmer		Miss	18.267	formerly of Portsmouth, at Cheltenham
Palmer		Capt	25.174	of Lewisham
Palmer	E	Miss	32.263	
Parish	John	Capt RN	33.351	
Parker	Eliza	Miss	3.516	
Parker	Hyde	Adm Sir	4.526	43 yrs older than his bride
Parker		Miss	6.434	daughter of Sir Peter Parker
Parker		Miss	7.532	of Arundel
Parker	Anne	Miss	14.511	
Parker	W G	RN, Sir	20.255	
Parker	Peter	Capt RN	21.264	
Parker	Mary	Miss	23.439	
Parker	William	Capt RN	23.519	
Parker		Major RA	32.439	at Sunning Hill
Parker		Lady	40.164	
Parkins		Mr	25.513	at Penzance
Parkins		Miss	26.264	at Plymouth
Parkinson		Capt RN	3.331	
Parkyns	Ann C	Miss	23.349	at Bermuda
Parr	Anna Maria	Miss	26.515	
Parry	Francis	Capt HEIC	4.527	
Parry	Mary Anne	Miss	29.511	
Parry	E	Lt	30.87	
Parry	Richard		30.175	
			30.359	
Parry	H	RN	34.352	
Parsons		Lt RN	1.347	
Parsons	C	Miss	26.264	
Pascoe		Mr	26.350	of Truro at Dover
Pasley		Miss	19.515	at Edmonton
Patch	Emma	Miss	34.439	
Patch	Charlotte	Miss	35.516	
Pater		Miss	31.438	at Madras
Paterson		Miss	9.251	at Chatham
Patrick		Miss	34.351	of Plymouth Dock
Patterson		Capt RN	5.280	
Patterson		Capt HEIC	6.348	at Strabane
Patterson		Lt RM	14.262	
Patterson	J	Capt HEIC	18.267	
Patterson		Lt RN	25.352	
Pattison		Miss	20.255	
Patton		Miss	10.175	
			10.263	
Patton	Anna	Miss	12.86	
			12.255	
Patton	J	Miss	18.267	daughter of the Governor of St Helena
Patton	Elizabeth	Miss	34.512	
Paul	Fanny	Miss	4.444	aged 13 to a man of 80
Paulett	Henry	R Adm Lord	30.447	
Pawrie	Sophia	Miss	28.439	
Paxton	Mary	Miss	30.87	
Payne	Ann	Miss	8.87	
Payne	M	Miss	23.440	

Payne Charles F	Capt RN	25.85	
Payne	Mr	26.178	of Portsmouth Dockyard
Payne	Miss	31.87	at Plymouth
Peacock	Miss	24.85	of Gibraltar at Kye, Lincs
Peake	Capt RN	16.175	
Peake Sarah	Miss	27.514	
Pearce	Miss	4.444	
Pearce R E	Miss	32.263	
Pearson Richard H	Capt	2.171	
Pearson Hannah	Miss	8.352	
Pearson Frances	Miss	22.440	
Pearson	Miss	26.178	of Dumfries, New Brunswick
Peirce Sophia	Miss	4.347	
Peirse Harriet E	Miss	34.176	
Pelbit	Lt	23.175	at Chatham
Pellew	Miss	10.350	
Pellew Frances	Miss	22.440	
Pellew Julia	Miss	23.87	
Pellew Fleetwood B	Capt RN, Hon	35.516	
Pellowe	Capt RN	14.262	
Pelly Charles	Capt RN	12.86	
Penford	Miss	12.255	at Ringwood
Pengelly	Lt RN	26.350	
Penn	Miss	34.439	
Penrose William		13.164	aged 74 to his grand niece of 21
Penrose Charlotte M	Miss	38.176	at Malta
Percival M	Capt RM	24.174	
Perdreau Stephen	Lt RN	8.176	
Peredic Mary	Miss	25.263	
Perfect	Miss	13.85	
Perkins	Miss	33.511	of Portsea
Perry Willam		12.511	
Pert Phoebe	Miss	19.439	
Petley H	Lt RN	6.516	
Petley	Lt RN	16.88	at Plymouth
Phelan C T		34.176	
Phelps Sarah	Miss	33.511	
Phillips	Capt RN	18.437	at Bath
Phillips	Miss	30.87	at Deal
Phipps W		28.438	
Pickernell	Lt RN	33.511	
Piddell	Mr	24.514	of Portsmouth
Pierrepont Augusta	the Hon	8.439	
Pigot G	Capt RN	26.87	
Pike Mary Anne	Miss	30.521	
Pinhorn F	Miss	17.352	
Pinnock	Miss	2.82	
Pipon E	Miss	13.504	at Jersey
Pipon Mary	Miss	32.176	at Jersey
Pipon	Capt	33.351	7th or Queen's Own Dragoons
Pitt Charles	Lt RN	24.514	
Pittman John	Reverend	33.511	
Pizzie	Miss	22.352	
Platt	Capt	23.264	Royal South Lincoln- shire Regiment of Militia
Pleydell S P		26.178	

Name	Title	Ref	Note
Plumer	Miss	13.335	
Plumley	Rev Mr	30.447	
Pocock	Capt	25.174	at Falmouth
Pole	Miss	8.176	daughter of Adm Sir Charles P.
Pollard Catherine	Miss	6.172	
Polyblank	Miss	26.178	at Stoke Ch, Plymouth
Popham Joseph L	Capt RN	5.544	
Popham	Miss	32.439	at Sunning Hill
Popplewell James		21.352	
Popplewell M J	Capt RN	34.439	
Poulett	Capt RN, Hon	26.515	
Powell P	Miss	1.540	
Powell Emily	Miss	29.263	
Poyntz Stephen	Capt RN	8.352	
Poyntz	Hon Miss	22.175	
Prescott	Capt RN	34.88	at Chelsea
Preston	Miss	16.264	
Prevost	Lt RN	1.174	
Prevost	Capt RN	31.262	at Chatham
Price James	Mr	3.420	
Price	Mr	18.83	at Kingston
Price John	Capt RN	33.351	
Price Caroline	Miss	33.351	
Prickard James	Capt RN	33.351	
Pridham R	Lt RN	5.280	
Pridham Mary	Miss	28.87	
Priestley	Miss	9.339	of Halifax
Pringle Margaret	Miss	24.514	
Pritchard J W	Lt RN	24.85	
Pritchard R D	Lt RN	24.85	
Proby	Miss	2.547	
Proby Elizabeth	Lady	35.175	
Proctor Alexander		2.448	
Proctor William B	Capt RN	27.438	
Prothery N P		1.540	
Proud Harriet	Miss	30.359	
Prowting Ann Mary	Miss	26.351	
Pryan	Doctor	23.350	
Prynn Jane	Miss	28.439	
Pullen	Lt RN	25.85	at Plymouth
Pullibank	Miss	28.262	aged 23
Pulling	Mrs	7.276	
Pulling George C	Capt RN	9.165	
Purchase J W	Lt RN	24.515	
Purve G	Miss	11.421	
Purvis	R Adm	12.165	
Purvis J B	Capt RN	34.512	
Purvis Renira C	Miss	34.512	
Putland	Mrs	24.438	nee Bligh, at Sydney N.S.W.
Pye	Miss	23.175	
Pym	Capt RN	7.452	
Pym	Miss	28.87	at Teignmouth
Pyne Richard C		22.352	
Pyne H	Lt RN	27.438	
Qualsh Ann	Miss	7.364	

Quelsh	Lt RN	9.251	
Raby	Miss	14.262	
Radford Alicia A	Miss	24.175	
Raigersfeld	Capt	7.180	
Raikes	Miss	1.347	
Rainier J S	Capt RN	15.264	
Rains	Mrs	19.176	at Ramsgate
Raison	Miss	4.444	
Raitt Charles		1.347	
Ramsbottom	Miss	9.497	of Windsor
Randall	Miss	7.452	
Ranwell	Miss	14.262	of Portsea
Ranwell William	Miss	29.439	
Rashleigh J S	Reverend	18.83	
Rathborne Wilson	Capt RN	14.511	
Ravenscroft W	Lt RM	12.86	
Ravenscroft Maria	Miss	30.447	
Rawbone	Miss	13.85	
Rawes	Capt HEIC	30.359	
		30.447	
Rawlings H	Miss	11.493	
Rawlins Frances G	Miss	29.87	
Rayner	Miss	24.174	at Dawlish
Rayner Anne	Miss	30.264	on Jersey
Reade Eliza	Miss	24.86	at Bengal
Reed Sophia B	Miss	30.175	
Reeves Maria	Miss	28.513	
Reed Richard R		32.263	
Reeves Sophia	Miss	22.520	
Reid	Miss	8.176	
Reid	Miss	18.174	
Remington T		16.175	
Renaud	Reverend	16.88	
Rennell	Miss	22.352	
Renwick	Lt RN	16.264	at Gosport
Reveley	Miss	1.261	
Reynolds	Capt RN	30.359	at Deal
Rich	Miss	20.255	at Sunning, Berks
Richards G S	Lt RN	31.352	
Richards Jenny C	Miss	32.439	
Richardson	Miss	18.267	of Berwick
Richardson	Mrs	18.519	widow of the late Capt R.
Richardson William	Lt RN	25.174	
Richdale	Major	28.438	of 70th Regmt
Ricketts George P		4.347	
Ricketts	Capt RN	7.452	
Rickford Thomas		27.86	
Rickman	Miss	27.438	of Deal
Rickman J	Lt RN	28.262	aged 78
Riffe de	Capt RN	34.352	at Gloster
Rivett Anna-Maria	Miss	33.176	
Roberts J R		26.351	
Roberts Elizabeth	Miss	29.87	
Roberts	Lt RN	32.262	
Robertson A	Miss	20.80	

Robertson Anne	Miss	29.511	
Robinson Mark	Capt RN	1.261	
Robinson	Miss	6.172	at Bishops Waltham
Robinson Ann	Miss	7.532	appears to have served in action on the La Seine, frigate, in Sgn's department
Robinson A	Miss	19.515	
Robinson Peter T	Major	23.439	8th or King's Owm Regiment
Rodd J Tremaine	Capt	22.352	
Rodney Frances E	Miss	24.86	at Colombo
Rogers	Miss	7.532	of Beaulieu near Southampton
Rogers	Mr	13.164	at Portsmouth
Rogers	Miss	28.176	at Plymouth
Rogers	Miss	30.359	of Lymington
Rogers Matainna	Miss	30.447	
Rogers Augusta-L	Miss	32.176	
		32.262	
Rolland	Capt HEIC	26.350	
Rolles R	Capt RN	6.516	
Rolles	Capt RN	13.85	
Rooke	Miss	26.264	of Salisbury
Rose John	Capt HEIC	25.263	
Ross James	Capt RN	2.171	
Ross	Lt RN	8.352	
Ross	Capt	10.175	
Ross Elizabeth	Miss	18.83	
Ross	Miss	25.513	of St Vincent's
Ross James	Capt HEIC	27.175	
Rouse J W	Lt RN	28.438	
Rowe Catherena	Miss	6.516	
Rowe Maria	Miss	8.176	
Rowe George	Surgeon RN	8.176	
Rowe M A	Miss	15.87	
Rowe	Mr	24.515	
Rowe	Lt RN	33.511	
Rowlands David	MD FRS	27.438	
Rowley Joshua	Reverend	1.446	
Rowley S C	Capt RN	14.350	at Kinsale
Rudall Mary	Miss	26.514	
Ruddle	Miss	5.96	
Rumbold	Lady	22.352	
Rundall	Miss	25.174	at Stoke Church, Plymouth
Rundle	Miss	33.351	of Lambeth
Russell John		27.175	
Russell	Lt RN	27.514	
Ruttenbury J F		24.85	
Ryves	Capt RN	15.264	
Sabine	Capt	4.168	of the Guards
St Aubyn James		14.350	at Lisbon
St Aubyn	Mrs	22.264	at Truro
St Barbe Ethelred	Miss	20.493	
St Croix Leonora	Miss	4.444	
St George	Col Hon	13.504	of Switzerland
St Leger	Miss	19.439	at Calcutta
Salmon H S	Miss	13.423	

Salmon	Miss	23.440	
Salter	Mr	23.175	
Saltwell Mary-Ann	Miss	21.352	
Samber	Miss	13.335	
Samuel	Miss	28.176	
Sandys S M	Capt RM	24.352	
Saumarez R		11.493	
Saumarez James	Reverend	32.351	
Saward Eliza	Miss	32.263	
Saxe	Duke of	35.239	
Saxe-Meiningen	Princess of	40.69	
Saxton	Miss	14.86	by special licence
Sayer George	Capt	2.263	
Scales	Miss	7.532	
Scarville Jane	Miss	1.261	
Schollar Elizabeth	Miss	26.86	
Schomberg	Miss	12.86	
Schultz G A	Lt RN	26.515	
Scobell Edward	Capt RN	35.352	
Scobell	Miss	38.176	
Scott Matthew H	Capt RN	2.82	
Scott	Miss	6.516	
Scott	Capt RN	24.438	at Bothwell Castle
Scott Octavius	Lt RM	28.263	
Scott	Lt	33.87	of HMS Tonnant at Halifax, Nova Scotia
Scott H		33.87	
Scott John	Capt RN	34.88	
Scott Isabella	Mrs	34.176	
Scott Edward T	Capt RN	35.263	by special licence
Scourfield Mary	Miss	1.446	
Scousby Arabella	Miss	27.351	of Whitby at Gosport
Sebire	Miss	8.176	of Guernsey
Senhouse	Capt RN	23.519	at Plymouth
Serrel	Capt RN	12.165	
Seton	Miss	14.511	
Seward	Capt RN	3.156	
Seymour Joseph		6.516	
Seymour G F	Capt Hon	25.439	
Seymour	Miss	32.511	at St Mary le bone Ch
Seymour F E	Capt RN	33.176	
Shank Henry	HEIC	20.166	
Shairp Christiana	Miss	8.439	
Sharp Edward		7.180	
Sheldon	Miss	17.520	of Portsmouth
Shepherd	Mr	26.178	at Stoke Church, Plymouth
Shepherd Mary	Miss	34.351	
Sheppard	Miss	14.350	at Plymouth
Sheriff Jane	Miss	19.263	
Sherriff	Capt RN	24.85	at Mary-le-bone
Shiells Thomas C		16.514	
Shier	Mr	23.440	of Portsea
Shirley	Mrs	1.261	
Shirley	Capt RN	3.240	
Shoredike Paul		30.447	

Shortland T G	Capt RN	2.644	
		3.156	
Shortland	Mrs	25.263	of Buckland
Shoveller T		15.176	
Shoveller	Mr	28.87	of Portsea
Shuldham	Lady	14.262	
Shuldt Elizabeth	Mrs	27.264	nee Tarrant
Shute Harriet	Miss	19.263	
Sidney Wm		26.515	
Silver Mary Francis	Miss	20.80	
Simpson	Capt RM	4.347	
Sinclair John G	Sir	27.514	
Sison William		27.175	
Sisron	Miss	7.532	
Skardon S	Miss	22.88	
Skene Alexander	Capt RN	31.352	
Skinner	Miss	25.513	at Gibraltar
		26.86	
Skottowe George		6.172	
Skyring	Mrs	24.85	nee Austen
Slade W		17.352	
Slade	Miss	28.513	of Plymouth
Sladen J B		20.493	
Slight J		28.439	
Slyman	Miss	4.347	
Smith Elizabeth	Miss	2.448	
Smith	Miss	5.96	grand-daughter of Capt James Smith of Beverley
Smith Louisa	Miss	7.92	
Smith	Lt RM	11.87	
Smith H W	Lt RN	12.165	
Smith	Lt & QM RM	14.511	
Smith	Miss	15.87	at Chatham(?)
Smith Charlotte	Hon	21.352	
Smith	Miss	22.264	eldest daughter of Col S. RM
Smith William S	R Adm Sir	22.352	
Smith Maria Emma	Miss	23.87	
Smith Ann	Miss	24.515	at Woolwich
Smith	Miss	24.515	at Woolwich (sister to Ann S.?)
Smith Elizabeth Ann	Miss	24.515	
Smith Matthew	Capt RN	26.350	
Smith	Lt RN	26.515	of HMS Zenobia
Smith	Miss	27.438	of Portsmouth at St Andrew's, Holborn
Smith Peter	MD RN	27.438	by special licence
Smith J William		29.511	
Smith George		32.351	
Smith Hannah	Miss	33.87	
Smith	Lt RN	34.439	of HMS Peruvian
Smith	Mr, Sgn RN	34.439	at Plymouth Dock
Smith Edw	Lt RN	34.440	
Smith Catherine	Miss	35.440	
Smith Charlotte J	Miss	38.87	
		38.88	
Smyth	Miss	5.375	niece of Sir Wm Smyth
Smyth	Miss	11.175	

Smythe Edward J		22.440	
Smythe Fredrica CUC	Miss	32.262	at Prince Edward Is, North America
Snell Elizabeth R	Miss	6.84	
Sneyd Clement	Capt RN	30.447	
Snook A	Miss	8.520	
Soady Mary	Miss	13.423	
Soady Sibella	Miss	26.178	
Sole	Miss	16.88	of Plymouth Dock
Somerville	Lt RN	26.350	
Somerville Mary	Miss	31.438	
Somerville Diana B	Miss	38.88	
Sorockin	Lt	30.175	Russian Navy, at Gravesend
South Harriet	Miss	34.440	
Sparg	Miss	14.262	of Penryn
Sparshott Daniel		8.520	
Spear Joseph	Capt RN	22.352	
		22.519	
Spearing M	Miss	14.511	
Spearing	Miss	19.86	at Greenwich
Speek W	Lt RN	32.439	
Spence H H	Capt RN	17.263	
Spencer John		26.350	
Spencer Mary-Ann	Miss	27.264	
Spencer Richard	Capt RN	28.263	
Spencer Jane	Miss	33.351	
Spengler Van	Capt	5.187	of the Dutch Navy
Spratt	Miss	6.434	in Calcutta
Spratt Maria	Miss	7.364	
Sprot Frances	Miss	18.437	
Sprott	Lt	18.174	at Edinburgh
		18.267	
Spry Harriet	Miss	3.240	
Stable Maria	Miss	11.87	
Stag	Miss	27.438	of Fratton
Stanbury Mary Ann	Miss	32.351	
Stanfell Francis	Capt RN	24.515	
Stanhope	Miss	18.83	at Wickham, Hants
Stanton E	Miss	16.175	
Stapleton J		6.172	of 20th Regmt of Foot
Stares Thomas (junior)		3.516	
Stedman	Capt	11.493	
Stedman Thomas		32.262	
Stephens	Miss	24.515	of Parson's Green
Stephens E	Lt RN	33.351	
Stevens Margaret-J		25.174	
Steward Ann	Miss	33.351	
Stewart	Miss	8.520	in Fifeshire
Stewart E	Miss	14.511	at Gibraltar
Stewers	Miss	24.438	
Stewart T	RN	24.351	
Stewart	Lt RN	25.263	
Stiles	Miss	30.447	at Plymouth
Stirling John		7.92	
Stoddart J	Doctor	10.175	
Stoddart Pringle	Capt	18.437	

Stokes	Miss	14.511	of Chepstow
Stone J C	Lt RN	13.423	
Stone Esther	Miss	38.88	
Stonestreet El'beth	Miss	19.439	
Stopford Robert	R Adm RN, Hon	22.88	
Stopford W	Lt RN	33.87	
Storie	Miss	1.261	
Stormar Jane	Miss	25.174	
Storry	Miss	26.264	at St Peter's, Colchester
Strachan Richard	V Adm Sir	27.438	
Stretton S		29.87	
Strickney S		33.511	
Strictland	Miss	32.351	of Portsea
Strover	Capt HEIC	27.86	
Strover Mary Ann		27.86	
Stuart	Capt RN	18.347	
Stuart John		26.87	
Stuart S H	Capt RN	34.440	
Stupart Gustavus	Capt RN	28.439	
Sturrock Henry	Capt HEIC	22.264	
Stuvang	Capt RN	13.245	
Sullivan O	Miss	11.87	
Sullivan	Miss	18.347	at Christchurch, Hants
Sullivan Thomas B	Capt	19.351	
Sumner Elizabeth M	Miss	24.438	
Supple William		12.86	
Surridge	Capt RN	17.263	
Suther	Mr	28.438	at Halifax
Sutton	Capt RN	15.351	at Bungay
Swaine S	Capt RN	16.264	
Swann Ann	Mrs	19.515	
Swayne Arabella E R	Miss	27.175	
Swetenham Ellen	Miss	30.447	
Swinders George		26.87	
Sykes	Miss	3.516	
Sykes	Miss	6.259	
Sykes John	Capt HEIC	20.493	
Sykes	Capt RN	25.513	at Edinburgh
Symes	Capt RN	33.511	
Symonds	Miss	8.352	
Symonds	Capt RN	33.264	at Fareham
Symons Julia	Miss	26.87	
Tadman A	Miss	25.440	
Tailor H	Capt RN	32.438	
Talbot Elizabeth T	Lady	11.421	
Talbot Mary	Lady	33.440	
Talbot John	Capt Sir	34.439	
Tappen Jemima	Miss	33.176	
		33.351	
Tatlock	Miss	23.350	
Taylor	Miss	14.262	in Malta
Taylor Mary	Miss	20.167	at Cape of Good Hope
Taylor Ann	Miss	26.515	
Taylor J		30.87	
Taylor Grace	Miss	30.447	

Tedley	Capt	8.176	Coldstream Guards
Temple John		1.446	changed name from Dicken in 1796
Temple Charlotte F	Miss	25.352	
Temple Francis	Capt RN	34.439	
Templer Charlotte-F	Miss	25.174	
Tessimond J		26.350	
Theisser	Miss	31.262	of Woodcote Pk, Surrey
Thickness(e)	Capt RN	3.420	
		3.516	
Thomas Thomas	Capt RN	6.434	in Calcutta
Thomas	Miss	10.438	
Thomas Ann	Miss	14.262	
Thomas	Miss	24.515	of Narbeth
Thomas J T R	Lt RN	29.87	
Thompson Thomas B	Capt RN, Sir	1.347	
Thompson	Miss	13.245	of Southwold
Thompson	Miss	14.350	of Cork
Thompson	Miss	18.519	of Kirby Hall
Thompson Margaret	Miss	19.515	
Thompson John		25.263	
Thompson Elizabeth	Miss	26.178	
Thompson	Miss	27.514	at Southampton
Thompson Maria	Miss	33.511	
Thompson F	Lt RN	34.440	
Thomson A	Miss	13.246	
Thornborough	R Adm	8.520	
Thornhill Wm	Capt	34.440	
Thorold	Miss	13.504	
Thrale	Miss	19.86	by special licence
Tickell John		23.519	
Tilstone Benjamin		26.350	
Timbrell James	Capt HEIC	25.263	at Bombay
		25.513	
Timmins J T		19.439	
Tingcombe	Miss	1.261	
Tinmouth N		34.440	
Tobin	Capt	11.493	
Todd	Miss	12.511	of Glasgow
Todd Catherine E	Miss	28.438	at Gottenburgh
Tomkins James	Capt	25.86	
Tomlin John		7.180	
Toms	Miss	4.168	
Tonkin(s) E	Miss	2.644	
		3.156	
Took Elizabeth	Miss	28.176	
Tooley Richard	Lt RN	19.86	
Townly C Hazwell		18.174	
Townshend James	Lord	29.511	by special licence
Townshend	Capt RN	33.87	
Townshend Elizabeth	Miss	34.511	
Towry G H	Capt RN	8.439	
Trace Elizabeth	Miss	40.332	
Tracey	Miss	27.174	
Trant Clarissa E	Miss	27.175	at Curacoa
Travers Charlotte	Miss	25.86	

Travers	Capt RN	33.351	at Yarmouth
Treeweek Caroline	Miss	22.88	
Tregonnell Helen	Miss	31.262	
Tremenheere Walter	Capt RM	7.364	
Trenerry	Miss	24.174	at Penryn
		24.351	
Trevenen	Mrs	16.264	at St Boniface, IoW
Trollope	Capt RN	29.263	
Trotter	Doctor	24.438	at Newcastle
Troubridge Thomas	Capt Sir	24.352	
Trowbridge	Miss	22.520	
Troy	Miss	9.165	of Chatham
Truscott	Capt RN	33.440	at Bermuda
Tucker	Miss	23.519	at Bermuda
Tucker	Miss	24.515	at Exeter
Tucker S	Miss	26.86	
Tucker Benjamin		27.86	
Tucker Tudor	Capt RN	27.514	at Antigua
Tucker R	Lt RN	34.440	
Tucket George J T	Hon	35.352	at Brussels
Tuckfield W		24.515	
Tuke Mary Jane	Miss	26.178	
Turkey	Miss	21.264	of Winterborne, Wilts
Turner John	Reverend	26.514	
Turner	Lt RN	28.263	
Turquand W	Mrs	11.493	
Tustin Anne E	Miss	26.350	
Tutley Sally	Miss	25.513	
Tuttiet John		30.264	on Jersey
Twynham W H		26.514	at Gibraltar
Tyler Caroline	Miss	38.87	
Tyndale Joseph	Lt RN	7.364	
Upton	Miss	23.439	of Cheriton Bishop
Vale Benjamin	Reverend	30.522	
Van Cortlandt Sophia Sawyer, Miss		32.351	
Vandeput	Mrs	6.172	
Varlo	Miss	17.263	of Southwick
Vazie Harriet	Miss	32.438	
Venour	Miss	34.352	at Gloster
Ventham	Miss	3.516	
Vincent	Capt RN	14.86	
Vincent R B	Capt RN	14.174	
Vivion	Miss	10.517	
Voller	Miss	26.514	
Wade Frederick G	Lt	26.87	of 25th Regmt of Light Dragns at Bangalore
Wade W P	Lt RN	29.351	
Waghorn Eliza	Miss	2.82	
Walcot Mathilda	Miss	24.514	
Waldegrave	Capt RN, Hon	28.87	
		28.176	
Waldegrave Emily	Hon Miss	34.352	
Walker	Lt RM	24.352	at Cambridge

Wallker E N	Miss	27.264	
Walker	Miss	28.263	of Cosgrove, Notts
Walker William		28.352	
Waller	Miss	6.516	at Sandwich
Wallis W	Lt RN	5.375	
Wallis	Miss	5.544	of Helston, Cornwall
Wallis Elizabeth	Miss	29.511	
Walpole	Lord	28.176	by special licence
Walsh Biddy	Miss	28.513	at St John's, Newfoundland
Walter Anne Maria	Miss	22.519	
Walter Elizabeth	Miss	24.263	
Walton Harriet	Miss	2.448	
Walton Jacob	Capt RN	22.520	
Walton Thomas T		28.438	at Gottenburgh
Ward	Capt RN	26.515	at Mitcham
Ward	Miss	28.263	at Marlborough
Wardrop James		32.176	
Waring Henry	Capt RN	13.335	
Waring T		28.262	
Warne	Miss	24.438	
Warre	Miss	4.526	
Warre	Miss	34.352	of Camden Town
Warren Mary	Miss	4.167	
Warren S		4.527	
Warren	Miss	8.176	daughter of Sir John B Warren
Warren C	Miss	8.352	at Calcutta
Warren	Capt RN	11.263	
Warren J F	Lt RN	30.447	
Warren Susan		34.439	
Wassenberg Christian Lewis		24.438	at Bombay
Watkins Harriet	Miss	35.86	
Watson	Mrs	24.174	nee Dudson, at Madras
Watson Eliza Ann	Miss	27.86	of Plymouth, married J Martin
Watson Eliza-Ann	Miss	27.175	married Wm Sison, at Greenwich
Watt Alexander		26.178	
Watts	Miss	6.84	of the Isle of Wight
Webb Jane	Miss	4.256	
Webb	Mr	14.262	at Portsea
Webb	Miss	25.85	late of Plymton, at Marksbury
Webb Mary Ann	Miss	30.522	
Webster Ann	Miss	13.164	to her 74 year old grand uncle
Webster Harriet	Miss	35.516	
Weekes	Miss	26.264	of Plymton
Welladvice	Mrs	22.264	of Charlton, Kent at St Mary-le-bone
Wells John	V Adm	33.511	
Wells W	Capt RN	35.175	
Welsford	Mr	1.261	
Welsford Frances A	Miss	27.86	
Welsh	Capt RN	13.245	
West James		24.351	
West C	Capt RN	34.352	
Westbrook Ann	Miss	7.452	
Westbrook Richard		28.439	
Westby N		34.352	

Westcott Mary Lott	Miss	24.175	
Westcott	Mr	29.352	at Honiton
Weyland Emma C	Miss	11.421	
Whapshare	Miss	4.526	
Whitbread J		22.264	
Whitbread	Miss	28.87	daughter of Samuel W. MP
		28.176	
Whitby	Capt	8.352	
Whitcher Charles		32.511	
Whitcomb Charles		30.175	
White	Miss	5.280	of Wallingswell
White S	Miss	17.352	
White	Mr	25.263	
White Martin	Capt RN	26.264	at Jersey
White Letitia-Mary	Miss	32.176	
White Susan	Miss	34.439	
White	Miss	34.440	of Bingham Town near Gosport
White J Chambers	Capt RN	35.440	
Whitelocke	Miss	8.176	
Whitmore Jane	Miss	21.519	
Whitmore	Miss	33.351	at Teignmouth
Whyte	Capt RN	9.423	
Widowfield	Miss	20.335	at Whitby
Wigg	Miss	8.439	
Wiles Jane	Miss	24.352	
Wilkins J H		24.263	at Bombay
Wilkinson	Capt RN	12.431	
Wilkinson J		22.520	
Wilks J B		26.87	
Willatts Julia-Ann		25.174	
Willes	Miss	9.497	
Willes G G	Capt	31.87	
Williams	Miss	2.644	
Williams Bridgman	Miss	4.526	
Williams Thomas	Capt RN, Sir	4.526	
Williams C D	Lt RN	11.87	
Williams	Miss	14.350	of Berwick Cas., Wilts
Williams	Capt RN	16.352	
Williams	Miss	16.352	of Canon Street
Williams Joseph		18.267	
Williams C W		20.493	
Williams Catherine	Miss	24.85	at Malta
Williams Daniel	Reverend	24.263	
Williams J		24.351	at Fowey
Williams		24.438	to Mary Gibbs
Williams William P		25.263	
Williams Ann		27.86	
Williams Frances	Miss	27.175	
Williams Charles		28.176	
Williams	Lt RM	28.352	at St Martin's in the Fields
Williams W		30.175	
Williams Elizabeth	Miss	32.263	
Williams David	Reverend	33.87	
Williams A F		33.176	at Gibraltar
Williams R	Capt RN	33.351	
Willins	Miss	2.644	

Willcock	Miss	10.87	of Bedford Square
Wills Sarah	Miss	25.440	
Willyams Cooper	Reverend	6.84	
Wilmot Jane	Miss	27.86	
Wilmott	Miss	16.264	
Wilson Thomas M	Sir	2.448	
Wilson A	Lt RN	4.526	
Wilson	R Adm	6.172	
Wilson Caroline	Miss	6.516	of Penrith at Plymouth
Wilson Mary Ann	Miss	21.444	
Wilson	Lt RN	24.174	at Penryn
		24.351	
Wilson	Miss	26.178	of Southsea, Portsmouth
Wilson Alicia M	Miss	28.513	
Wilson	Mrs	29.351	of Marlborough at Walmer, Kent
Wilson	Capt RN	38.88	of Stow near Kendal
Windle Maria	Miss	28.513	
Wingrove G P	Capt RM	15.87	
Wingrove Ann	Miss	34.440	
Wining	Lt RN	28.87	at Ryde, IoW
Winkworth Elizabeth	Miss	30.175	
		30.359	
Winthrop	Capt RN	13.85	
Wise W F	Capt RN	23.519	
Wise S		29.352	
Wiseman William	Capt Sir	28.438	at Bagdaad
Wishart Ross	Miss	27.86	
Wodehouse Philip	Hon	32.87	at Halifax, Nova Scotia
		32.262	
Wolley Thomas	Capt RN	11.343	
Wood Charlotte	Miss	4.526	
Wood Eliza	Miss	15.87	
Wood Marianne	Miss	19.176	of Manchester at Mary-le-bone Church
Wood Eliza	Miss	30.175	
Wood	Mrs	36.86	at Bermuda
Woodgate	Miss	8.439	
Woodhouse Elizabeth	Miss	27.514	
Woodley	Miss	34.352	at Bloxworth, Devon
Woodriff Caroline E	Miss	29.511	
Woolcombe Henry	Reverend	27.351	
Woolcombe John M		27.351	
Wooldridge	Capt	7.532	
Wooldridge	Capt RN	22.88	
Woolward John	Lt RN	26.514	of Ramsgate at Greenwich
Wordsworth	Miss	16.174	
Worship	Mrs	21.87	of Runham, Norfolk
Worwood	Mrs	19.86	of Headington at St George's, Hanover Sq.
Worth Sophia	Miss	12.431	
Wright	Miss	16.175	of Harling Hall, N'folk
Wright William		29.174	
Wyborn Bargrave	Lt	9.165	of 18th Dragoons
Wyke Alicia	Miss	30.447	
Wynch G	Mrs	13.85	

Wynne	Capt RN	11.263	
Yates	Miss	6.172	at Plymouth
Yates F	Miss	7.452	
Yates	Capt HEIC	19.439	at Calcutta
Yates	Miss	29.439	of Southampton
Yeates	Miss	5.280	
Yorke Caroline	Lady	26.438	
Yorke Joseph S	R Adm Sir	29.439	by special licence
Young	Capt RN	7.532	
Young	Capt RN	8.87	at Gibraltar
Young E	Lt RM	13.85	
Young T	Capt RM	13.85	
Young	Mr	24.515	
Young Frances B	Miss	25.86	
Young	Capt RN	28.87	at Cork
Young Emma	Miss	29.174	
Younghusband	Miss	17.176	at Alverstoke

DEATHS

Aalbers N S	Capt	17.341	
Abbott R		32.511	
Accool		24.74	a Lascar
Achison Arthur	Capt RN	39.498	
Ackenhead John		14.437	see also Aikenhead, J
Acton William		33.79	
Adair Charles W	Capt RM	14.437	
Adair William		16.81	
Adam	Mrs	1.262	wife of William Adam, only dau of John, Earl of Wigton
Adam	Mr	11.494	
Adams Francis		4.444	
Adams Robert		25.514/5	a Purser of Portsmouth, former shipbuilder at Buckler's Yard
Adams	Mr	26.87	Purser RN
Adams Jacob	Lt RN	36.87	
Adams Alexander		38.348	
Adamson Cuthbert	Lt	12.432	
		12.511	
Adamson J	Lt RM	36.440	
Adkin Nathaniel		30.248	
Adye J M	Capt RN	37.176	
Affleck Philip	Adm	2.644	
Affleck	Lady	2.644	widow of Adm Sir E Affleck
		3.80	
Affleck T	Capt RN	15.87	
Aikenhead John		14.437 ⎤	both described as Midshipmen
Aikenhead Thomas		15.118 ⎦	on the Royal Sovereign
Ainton William		29.348	
Alcock Clement		15.257	
Aldham G		30.84	
Aldridge William		29.78	
Alexander	Mr	21.352	surgeon of the Wanderer
Alexander Thomas		26.88	
Allcock	Lt RM	3.240	
Allcott	Lt RN	20.336	
Allen	Capt	2.548	of the Termagant
		2.644	
Allen John Carter	Adm	4.348	
Allen John		7.85	
Allen John		8.264	
Allen Samuel		25.341	
Allen Elizabeth	Mrs	26.180	
Allen	Lt	26.264	Governor of the Naval Knights of Windsor
Allen Griffith	Capt RN	32.511	
Allwright Thomas	Capt	9.166	
Alms	Mrs	22.440	widow of Capt J Alms
Alms	Mrs	34.352	wife of Admiral Alms
Alms James	V Adm RN	35.516	
Amelia Princess	HRH the	24.438	
Amyott J G		32.176	
Anderson John	Doctor	21.88	
Anderson	Mrs	21.176	wife of Capt A Anderson RM
Anderson James		22.504	

Name	Rank	Ref	Note
Anderson	Mr	25.88	late surgeon RN
Anderson Adam		33.340	
Anderson Alexander	Capt RM	33.88	
		33.257	
Anderson John	Capt RN	34.512	
Andrews George	Capt RN	24.175	
Andrews George	Lt RN	39.494	
Angus John	Mr	25.263	
Annard R		33.262	
Ansevan Andrew		27.511	
Anstruther C	Lt RN	32.264	
Anthony Walter		16.176	
Aplin	Mrs	25.176	wife of Adm Aplin
Aplin Peter	Adm	37.440	
Apthorp	Capt RN	12.432	
Archbold	Lt Col RM	21.87	
Archer Letitia	Miss	39.176	
Archdeacon	Mr	10.175	Purser of the Emerald
Armnecht	Mr	19.264	assistant surgeon
Armstrong J		19.176	
Arnold John		2.448	
Arnold William		5.280	
Arnold	Lt RN	26.87	
Arnold James		28.359	of the US frigate Chesapeake
Arnott James		18.267	
Arscott James	Lt RN	36.352	
Arthur William		29.175	Purser of the Armada
Arthur William	Lt RN	35.176	of Newcastle-upon-Tyne
Arthur	Mrs	39.498	
Artis Richard		31.257	
Ash W		33.262	
Ashbridge R S	Lt RM	27.507	
Ashford	Lt RN	26.179	of the Centaur
Ashley Thomas		20.253	
Ashley James	Lt RN	39.264	
Ashlington John	Lt RN	13.335	
Ashman Richard		15.257	
Ashmore Samuel	Capt RM	36.352	
Ashton Timothy		24.165	
Ashworth John		22.251	
Askew	Lt	12.511	of the Triumph
Astell	Capt	27.439	of the Margaret
Atcheson	Mr	7.529	Mid on the Temeraire
Atkins Thomas		22.251	
Atkinson George		28.88	
Atkinson William	Capt	29.264	
Atwell Thomas		33.352	
Aufrere Charles	Lt RN	2.548	
Auld	Lt RN	9.423	
Ausleck	Mr	18.520	of the Boreas
Austin	Mrs	32.352	wife of Capt Charles Austin
Austin Sylvester	Lt RN	35.264	
Avery	Lt RN	9.81	of the Chichester
Aylmer	Mrs	22.88	wife of Admiral Aylmer
Aylmer John	Adm	36.87	
Ayscough James	Capt RN	19.515	

Babington James	Lt RN	19.264	
Babington A G		25.87	
Bache	Mrs	30.448	wife of Capt Bache
Bachop James	Capt	2.263	
Badcock W R		20.494	
Bagley George		26.258	
Bagnell/Bagnold J	Lt RM	28.439	
Bagot Hervey		35.176	
Bagster D	Mrs	12.166	
Bagwell	the Hon Mrs	9.251	eldest daughter of Admiral Lord Graves
Baikie Hugh	Capt RN	36.174	
Bailey	Mrs	17.520	wife of Mr Bailey, Royal Navy Academy, Portsmouth
Baillie	Mrs	7.180	wife of Alexander Baillie, RN
Baillie Ross	Lady	39.87	
Bailward Henry M		28.88	
Baily	Capt RN	9.81	Senior Captain, Greenwich Hospital
Baines	Capt RN	24.176	at Carmarthan
Bakebury Henry		26.174	
Baker	Capt	12.87	of the Pelican
Baker J E	Lt	13.335	
Baker	Lt	15.264	of the Cerebus
Baker Henry	Mr	25.352	
Baker William		28.348	
Baker	Mr	29.88	Purser of the Magnet, a native of Portsea
Baker R		34.88	
Balderstone	Capt	20.494	of the Parthian
Balfour James		2.448	
Balfour Wm	Capt RN	36.174	
Balfour George R F		38.176	
Ball Daniel	Mr	1.176	
Ball Levi		18.520	
Ball Matthew	Mr	21.520	
Ball John Alexander	R Adm Sir	22.520	
Ballard S	Capt	18.520	infant son
Ballard	Capt RN	28.513	infant son, at Gosport
Bandwell Joseph		25.432	
Barbe John S	Capt RN	35.176	
Barber William		8.520	
Barber W		9.81	
Barber Walter		25.434	
Barber John		29.258	
Barber Robert		31.257	
Barfoot J	Capt HEIC	17.520	
Barglehole John		28.166	
Barker George		12.413	
Barker William		17.347	
Barker	Mrs	22.440	wife of Capt George Barker
Barker	Lt	23.352	of the Hussar
Barker Marshall		31.440	
Barlow W		26.180	
Barlow Elizabeth	Mrs	35.264	
Barlow	Mrs	38.348	wife of Sir Robert Barlow

Barnes John		14.262	
Barnes John		18.348	of the Renommee
Barnes	Mr	18.520	of the Boreas
Barnes Edward		19.342	
Barnes Thomas		28.82	
Baron John	Reverend	35.440	
Barr Thomas		30.85	
Barrington Samuel	Adm the Hon	4.168	
Barrington John		25.434	
Barron	Comm	25.88	of the Chesapeake
Barrow	Mrs	30.176	mother of W Barrow
Barry	Lt	18.240	of the 87th Regmt
Barry Thomas		30.85	
Barry	Lt RM	37.434	
Barter William		15.121	
Bartlett	Mr	3.156	at Woolwich
Bartlett Peter		29.258	
Barwell	Mr	13.246	of the Abergavenny
Barwell	Mrs	33.352	wife of Capt H Barwell
Basden	Mrs	23.352	see also Mrs D Ellison, wife of Capt Basden and 2nd daughter of Capt Jos. Ellison
Baskerville P	Capt	31.512	
Bass	Capt RN	23.176	of the Gluckstadt
Bassan	Lt RN	26.87	
Basset D	Lt	40.84	
Bassett	Mr	25.513	of Portsea
Bastard Edmund		37.264	
Bastol	Mr	24.515	Mid of the Pearlen
Batchelor Philip		27.506	
Bateman William		21.342	
Bates Joah		2.83	
Bates John James	Lt RN	29.257	
		29.264	
Bateson H	Lt	13.504	
Batt	Capt	14.350	of the Albatross
Batten John		34.512	
Battersby R H	Capt RN	36.518	
Battershell	Mr	27.87	Harbourmaster, Portsmouth
Battier G	Mr	13.86	late of Cook's Resolution
Battle	Corp RM	32.163	
Baufey B	Lt	19.88	
Bawden James	Capt	5.356	
Bawker Heindrick		28.162	
Baxter	Mr	29.264	asst surgeon of the Milford
Baxter	Lt RM	36.259	of the Leander
Bayley	Mr	2.155	Mid on the Amelia
Bayley	Mrs	11.263	widow of T Bayley
Bayley William		24.516	
Baylis Robert	Mr	1.88/175	
Bayly		4.444	the only son of Capt the Hon Paget Bayly
Bayly Paget	Capt RN	12.432	
Bayly	Miss	14.262	daughter of Mr Bayly of the Royal Academy, Portsmouth

Bayne		15.87	female relative of Capt William Bayne
Baynes T	Capt RN	39.176	
Bazely John	Adm	21.352	
Beach	Mr	16.440	master of the metal mills, Portsmouth Dockyard
Beard W	Lt RN	31.511	
Beat James		29.78	
Beatty Robert		33.340	
Beaufoy	Lt RN	18.520	
Beaver Philip	Capt RN	30.176	
Beazley Robert	Mr	39.423	
Bechinoe	Mrs	12.511	mother of Duchess of Roxburgh and sister to Sir J Smith
Beddeck Betsey	Miss	28.263	
Beddek W Stiles		2.448	
Beddick	Miss	19.88	
Bedford John		18.437	
Bedford	Mrs	19.439	widow of John Bedford
Bedford Charles	Master	30.360	
Bedford John	Capt RN	32.263	
Beecher William	Lt	25.87	
Bell James	Mid	5.356	on the Polyphemus
Bell James		14.258	seaman of the Phoenix
Bell	Mrs	27.176	wife of Capt Stephen Bell
Bell John		31.257	
Bell	Mr	34.176	of the Tagus
Bellamy Joseph		6.260	
Bellamy	Lt	12.432	of the Carysfort
		13.164	
Bellamy John	Capt	40.332	
Bellas Robert		2.644	
Bellaul		24.74	a Lascar
Belli George L	Lt	17.432	
Belson Joseph	Mr	1.262	
Belton John		31.426	
Benbow John		15.264	
Benge	Capt RN	33.512	
Bengle H		9.251	
Bennet Robert		2.439	
Bennet I A	Capt Hon	28.263	
Bennett Christ		26.83	
Bennett R N A		31.352	
Bennicke W		28.513	
Bentinck Albert A		20.424	
Bentinck John A		20.424	
Bentinck William	V Adm	29.352	
		30.88	
Benyon Charles	Lt RN	24.515	
Beresford	Lady	30.176	wife of Sir John Beresford
Beresford Marianne	Miss	40.244	
Beriff Robert C	Lt RN	36.87	
Berilles William		30.85	
Berkeley S E	Miss	13.166	
Berkeley	Lt Col RM	24.87	
Berkeley George C	Adm Sir	39.264	

Berkely V C	Capt	11.421	
Berry	Mr	6.157	Mid on the York
Berry Richard		16.81	
Berry William		22.259	
Bertie	Mrs	13.246	wife of R Adm Bertie
		13.335	
Bertie Catherine B	Miss	19.352	
Bertie Willoughby	Capt Hon	25.87	
Bertie Alex		27.506	
Bertie Willoughby	Capt Hon	28.263	his postumous son
Besborough G		14.350	
Best Richard		6.147	
Beswick	Mr	18.174	of the Arab
Betson Henry		13.410	
Bettesworth W A		14.512	
Bettesworth E B	Capt	19.420	
		19.440	
Betty Z	Mr	13.335	
Beurhemor	Mr	5.361	of the French Navy
Bevians	Lt RN	6.435	
Bewick John	Lt	31.503	
Bickerton	Lady	26.264	widow of Adm Richard B.
Bickerton James		27.345	
Bickhuss William		15.258	
Bicknels Charles H	Mr	1.446	
Bidden	Mr	16.347	Mid on the Monarch
Biddulph C	Capt RN	34.440	
Biggs Robert	V Adm	10.87	
Biggs Thomas		20.424	
Billiars Jane	Mrs	34.352	
Billinghurst	Lt RN	15.176	
Billinghurst	Lt RM	15.440	
Billinghurst T		32.511	Sgn of the Penelope
Billinghurst	Mr	33.176	Sgn of the Venerable
Binstead Thomas		12.432	
Birch Edward	Lt	3.516	
Birch	Lt RN	4.168	of the Triumph
Birchall	Mrs	15.176	wife of Capt Birchall
Birchall	Mrs	26.88	wife of Capt Birchall
Bird	Lt RM	8.352	at Bombay
Bird	Dr	13.85	
Bishop Charles C		20.80	
Bishop Robert W		24.87	
Bishop James		33.166	
Bishop W		37.86	
Bissel Maurice B		21.264	
Bissett G J P	Lt RM	36.259	
Biston William	Dr	5.376	
Blachford Barrington PMP		35.516	
Black J	Lt RN	9.497	
Black John		26.433	
Blackwood	the Hon Mrs	8.439	wife of Capt Blackwood
Blair	Dr	9.81	
		9.165	
Blair Ralph		17.343	
Blair Peter		29.258	

Blake	Capt RN	10.175	
Blake James		28.82	
Blanc le	Lt RN	26.179	of the Fearless
Bland Loftus O	Capt RN	24.87	
		24.175	
Blankett	R Adm	6.516	
Blaxton	Lt	7.92	
Bligh	Mrs	18.268	wife of Capt John Bligh RN
Bligh William	V Adm	38.511	
Blissett	Mr	25.513	of Portsea
Bloye Henry		31.348	
Bluett Ann	Mrs	24.88	
Blythe	Capt	30.360	of the Boxer
Blythe J		31.439	
Boger Coryndon	Capt RN	11.421	
Boger	Mrs	39.423	wife of Admiral Boger
Bogle Patrick		25.433	
Bogue J B	Capt RN	17.352	
Bogue John		29.257	
		29.264	
Bois du	Capt	15.264	of the French Navy
Boisrond	Major RM	14.511	
Bokman Nicholas		15.258	
Bolingbroke George		25.515	
Bolt Joseph	Capt RN	24.438	
Bolton Thomas	V Adm Lord	18.174	
Bolton Dennis	Lt RN	39.176	
Bomb Caspar		28.162	
Bommell Charles		16.81	
Bond William		15.258	
Bones James		6.260	
Bonley W	Lt RN	24.438	
Boone Susan	Mrs	38.88	
Booth Walter	Capt RN	23.352	
Borda Charles		2.171	
Boscawen William		25.513	
Boston	R Adm	20.80	
Bouch Jacob		29.348	
Bouchier	Capt RN	21.87	
Bougainville	Count de	26.264	
Bounton John	Lt RN	14.258	
Bourke	Mrs	29.512	at Chichester
Bourmaster John	Adm	18.520	
Boveard Charles		30.360	
Bovel Edward S		29.440	
Bover	Miss	23.88	daughter of Capt John Bover
Bowater Bridget	Mrs	27.439	
Bowater John	Lt Gen RM	30.360	
Bowditch Stephen		7.92	
Bowditch Samuel	Lt RM	25.264	
Bowdler John		2.263	
Bowen George		4.168	
Bowen	Miss	21.520	daughter of Commissioner James Bowen
Bowen George		23.520	
Bowen Richard	Lt	24.352	

Bowen Essex	Capt RN	26.88	
Bowen William	Capt RN	29.264	
Bowen James	Capt RN	29.512	
Bowen Robert C		36.258	
Bower Richard	Lt	24.440	
Bower Edmund		26.264	
Bowes William		29.502	
Bowes John		30.170	
Bowler John		20.256	
Bowles	Mr	18.268	of the Java
Bowyer George	Sir	4.527	
Bowyer	Mrs	27.440	mother of Capt Bowyer
Box George	Lt RN	25.175	
Boyd James	Lt	3.516	
		4.168	
Boyd W	Lt	11.494	
Boyd William		31.425	
Boyd George		37.168	
Boyer	Mrs	12.255	wife of R Adm Boyer
Boyes J D		14.512	
Boyle J	R Adm	25.88	
Boyle Charlotte	Miss	36.87	
Boyles Charles	V Adm	36.440	
Boys C W	Capt RN	23.88	
Boys Henry	Capt RN	36.518	
Bozier William		21.438	
Brabazon Lambert	Capt RN	25.352	
Brace Uppington	Mr	13.164	Surgeon RN
Brachio Guestn		25.346	
Bradby James	Capt	6.172	
Bradby Charlotte M	Miss	6.260	
Bradley P	Mrs	8.440	
Bradley	Adm	22.264	
Bradley	Mrs	26.351	wife of Capt John B., RN
Bradley William		30.240	
Bradshaw E	Mrs	5.188	wife of F Bradshaw
Bradshaw Eleanor	Miss	27.439	
Brady John		32.512	
Bragg William	Mr	21.264	
Braine James	Mr	39.88	
Brand	Lt RN	31.87	at Halifax
Brand	Mr	34.176	at Portsea
Branston	Lt RM	1.88	
		1.176	
Brass Hendrick		20.250	
Brassey Nathaniel		9.166	
Braithwaite R	Adm	14.86	
Brathwaite	Mrs	4.444	wife of Adm Brathwaite
Brasson Cornelius		25.432	
Braund Thomas		14.429	
		14.437	
Brawn Ernest		13.504	
Bray Joseph		16.81	
Bray	Mrs	24.440	wife of Mr Bray of Sheerness Dock yard
Bray James		28.352	see Vol 2 page 620

Bray	Lt	**29**.84	of the Plumper
Brazil William		**15**.434	
Brazil John		**25**.433	
Breamer John		**8**.334	
Bredon	Capt RM	**3**.420	
Brenton	R Adm	**7**.180	
Brenton John Jervis		**38**.348	
Brenton	Lady	**39**.263	wife of Sir Jahleel B.
Brett Charles	Mr	**1**.348	
Brewer Peter		**28**.169	
Brice	Mrs	**31**.176	wife of Capt Brice RN
Brice Arthur Hill	Major	**37**.440	aged 85 years
Bridge Richard	Lt RN	**39**.263	
Bridges	Mrs	**25**.264	wife of Capt Bridges
Bridges Brook John	Reverend	**28**.88	
Bridgman	Lt RN	**5**.188	
Brien Daniel		**27**.506	
Bright T	Lt RN	**10**.350	
Brine James	Adm RN	**32**.512	
Brio Antonio del		**24**.164	
Brisbane	Mrs	**12**.511	widow of Capt W B. RN
Brisbane John	Adm	**18**.520	
Brisbane T S J		**27**.176	
Brisbane	Mrs	**37**.440	widow of John Brisbane
Bristow William		**6**.157	
Britain J	Mr	**11**.494	
Brock H F	Lt	**27**.440	
Brocklesby Daniel		**6**.158	
Brocksopp Edward		**6**.172	
Broderip	Lt RN	**25**.515	of the Arachne
Brodie T C	Capt RN	**25**.440	
Brodie Alexander		**28**.166	
Brodie Joseph	Capt RN	**36**.87	
Broke H E	Miss	**34**.88	
Bromley	Mrs	**36**.518	wife of Edward Bromley
Brompton Alexander	Lt RN	**22**.352	
Brookbank John		**15**.257	
Brooke William		**25**.87	
Brooking J S		**28**.513	
Brooks Edward F		**14**.437	
Brooks	Mr	**15**.429	Mid of the Revenge
Brooks Thomas		**25**.433	
Brougiere	Mr	**20**.494	a Purser
Browell	Mrs	**9**.251	
Browell	Mrs	**22**.264	wife of Lt Governor of Greenwich Hospital
Brown	Capt	**1**.175	of the Kite, sloop of war, murdered at Sheerness
Brown John	Capt	**6**.348	
Brown John		**15**.258	seaman of the Atlas
Brown John		**16**.350	
Brown John		**16**.350	seaman on the Sheldrake
Brown Henry		**18**.345	seaman of the Hydra
Brown	Lt	**19**.88	of Bienfaisant, prison ship
Brown Thomas		**19**.259	
Brown John	Adm	**19**.440	

Brown		Mr	24.352	Sgn of the Magnet
Brown		Mr	24.439	Sgn HEIC
Brown Robert		Capt	25.263	of the American ship, Hindostan
Brown Isaac			27.345	
Brown Henry			28.348	
Brown William			28.348	
Brown William			29.78	of the Macedonian
Brown John			29.257	of the Amelia
Brown George			29.258	
Brown Joseph			30.85	AB on the Shannon
Brown Robert			31.257	
Brown Joseph		Pte RM	32.163	killed at Oswego
Brown J			32.176	Master of the Royal Charlotte
Brown		Mr	33.83	Asst Sgn, Plymouth
Brown Andrew		Capt	40.500	
Browne		Lt RN	2.83	Commander of the Urchin
Browne Richard		Capt RN	8.88	
Browne Charles		Lt RN	24.175	
Browne Benjamin			25.87	
Browne William		R Adm RN	32.439	
Browne William		Lt RN	35.86	
Browne Wm		Mr	39.88	
Brownrigg		Capt	15.264	of the Dart
Bruce		Mr	3.331	Bo'sun of the Arundel
Bruce		Mrs	6.172	wife of Lt L D Bruce
Bruce		Lt	9.251	of the Emerald
Bruce R			13.86	
Bruce William			15.434	
Bruce James			18.347	
Bruce		Capt	25.264	of the James
Bruce		Miss	26.88	
Bruce		Mrs	40.84	mother of Mrs Adm Fraser
Bruff		Mrs	24.352	wife of P S Bruff
Bruix		Adm	13.335	of the French Navy
Bruton N		V Adm	32.440	
Bryan William			15.434	
Bryan Michael			20.418	
Bryan		Capt RN	34.176	at Helston
Brydges Grey M			27.515	
Buchan E W		Lt	32.352	
Buchanan		Capt RN	7.452	of the Haarlem
Buchanan		QM	18.240	of the 87th Regmt
Buchanan		Mrs	25.88	wife of Capt Robert B.
Buchanan William		Surgeon	39.176	
Bucke T B		Lt	1.175	
Buckland John		Lt RM	25.87	
Buckle		Mrs	19.263	widow of Adm Buckle
Buckner Charles		Adm	25.176	
			25.264	
Budd Bonnell		Mr	23.440	
Budge William			26.180	
Bulcure Dennis			16.439	
Bull William			27.345	
Bullen		Mrs	39.423	mother of Capt Chas B., RN CB
Buller John St A			2.448	

Buller A	Lt	14.262	
Bulley George	Capt RN	39.87	
Bumford	Major RM	31.352	at Chatham
Bunbridge William		16.349	
Buntin Thomas		25.432	
Bunton	Lt	20.424	of the Audacious
Burchell Wm	Lt RN	32.440	
Burdett	Mrs	10.175	wife of Capt Burdett
Burdford William		25.264	
Burdon H L	Miss	16.88	
Burdon	Mrs	24.263	wife of Lt Chas Burdon
Burdon	Mrs	39.498	wife of Capt Burdon RN
Burdwood J		11.494	
Burges W	Capt RM	29.175	
Burgess	Mrs	6.84	widow of Capt Burgess
Burgess	Capt HEIC	18.437	
Burke Walter	Lt	6.172	
Burn John	Capt RN	29.176	
Burne Samuel	Capt RM	6.516	
Burne	Mr	29.175	Purser of the Cyane
Burnell William		37.264	
Burney Edward		26.88	
Burnside R		26.440	
Burrard Harry		22.352	
Burrell	Capt	18.240	of the 9th Light Drag
Burridge Edward		21.344	
Burrowes	Capt	16.349	of the Constance
Burt Robert		33.340	
Burt George	Lt RN	33.352	
Burton George	Capt	33.512	aged 89, of Trinity House
Burton George	Sir	35.175	
Bury Jane	Miss	28.440	
Busey John		3.311	
Bush	Mr	18.348	father of Lt Bush RN
Bush	Mrs	34.440	wife of Lt Bush RN
Bushby John	Capt RN	24.264	
Bushell George		23.170	
Busigny Simeon	Capt RM	14.437	
Busigny	Capt RM	14.512	of the Temeraire
Busk W de	Lt RN	10.350	
Butcher	Lt RN	39.263	
Butler Thomas		3.331	
Butt Peter		3.240	
Butt	Capt RN	11.263	his infant daughter
Butterfield E'beth	Mrs	9.166	
Butterfield	Mrs	11.263	wife of Capt B'field
Butterfield Elizabeth Anne,Miss		24.87	
Butterfield Althamiah Jane, Miss		32.352	
Butterfield Jane	Miss	32.440	
Buxton John		31.257	
Byan W	Capt RN	36.87	
Byers Robert		24.424	
Byng Elizabeth	Mrs	24.263	
Byng John		28.176	at Trichnopoly
Byron Edward	Reverend	26.440	

Name	Rank/Title	Reference	Notes
Caird David		40.74	
Caffrae Alexander		6.260	
Calcombe John		21.343	
Caldecott	Mrs	27.176	mother of Mrs Stevenson of Royal Naval Hosp, Haslar
Calder Robert	Adm Sir	40.243	
Caldwell James		22.504	
Caley Richard	Lt RN	2.548	
Callaghan James		22.505	
Callahan John James	Lt	22.250	
		22.352	
Callander Robert		30.360	
Callaway J		13.86	
Callaway Edwin	Lt RN	29.512	
Callaway Charles		33.166	
Calmady Charles HE	Adm	17.263	
Calthorp	Mr	36.259	Mid on the Leander
Calvert Anthony		20.424	
Camelford Thomas	Lord	11.263	
Cameron	Lt	12.511	of the Fly
Cameron	Mr	13.246	of the Diana
Cameron	Capt	23.176	of the Hazard
Campbell Patrick	Capt RN	2.263	
Campbell John		2.644	
Campbell Duncan	Capt RN	3.420	
Campbell Anne	Mrs	4.528	widow of S Brown, sgn RN
Campbell	Mr	17.176	foreman rigger, Portsmouth
Campbell Duncan		22.88	
Campbell Dugald	Major Gen RM	22.352	
Campbell G		25.87	
Campbell	Lt Col	25.256	of the 33rd Regmt
Campbell D		25.352	surgeon RN
Campbell James		27.506	
Campbell J	Capt	31.439	commander of Three Friends
Campbell John		31.503	landman of the Berwick
Campbell	Mrs	33.352	wife of Capt Donald Campbell
		33.440	
Campbell Robert	Capt RN	34.440	
Campbell John	Lt RM	39.264	
Canes	Mrs	17.440	widow of Capt E Canes
Cannadine Abraham		25.176	
Cannon	Mr	25.513	of Portsmouth
Cannon Augustus	Lt RN	29.82	
		29.175	
Cannon R	Lt RN	34.88	
Carborne	Lt RN	36.87	
Card John		29.78	
Card Thomas		29.348	
Cargell John		13.410	
Carleton Charles	the Hon	2.83	
Carlisle Sarah	Mrs	10.517	
Carmichael Douglas		22.505	
Carmody Cornelius		16.79	
Carnegie James L	Capt RN	32.440	
Carp	Captain	11.410	of the Atalanta
Carpenter	Capt RN, Hon	10.263	

Carpenter	Capt RN	27.176	a son of
Carpenter	Lt RN	31.439	of the Algerine
Carpenter	Mrs	35.264	at Stoke nr Plymouth
Carr	Lt	11.263	of Greenwich Hospital
Carr	Mr	25.440	Surgeon's mate of the Surrey, HEIC
Carr Robert	Lt RN	27.87	
Carra John		2.247	
Carrington James		22.250	
Carrington Gordon		22.251	
		22.352	
Carrington G W H		36.86	
Carrol	Lt	31.88	in Spain
Carroll John		26.433	
Carrow	Mr	32.264	master of the Statira
Carruthers Robert		2.83	Surgeon RN
Carruthers	Capt RN	5.376	
Carruthers Walter	Capt RM	24.263	
Carruthers	Mrs	24.264	widow of Gen Carruthers RM
Carter Hope		6.435	of the Centurion
Carter Louisa	Miss	24.440	
Carter Simon		29.258	
Carter H	Reverend	29.264	
Carter Eliza	Miss	32.440	
Carter Robert	Capt RN	39.424	
Carteret	Capt RN	27.352	of the Niaid
Cartwright	Capt RM	5.464	
Cartwright W P	Capt	14.262	Marine Battn, Bengal
Cartwright	Mrs	14.262	wife of previous entry
Cartwright Thomas		34.352	
Case Joseph		22.251	
Casey Edward		21.438	
		21.520	
Castries de	Marshal	3.240	former French Minister of Marine
Casumaty Anthony		25.432	
Cathcart	Capt Hon	12.255	eldest son of Lord Cathcart
Cattano Joseph		28.166	
Caulfield	Lt	19.352	of the Impereuse
Cavanagh James		15.259	
Caverton Thomas		26.180	
Cavill C	Lt RN	37.176	
Cayley William		5.96	
Cecil T W	Capt	32.511	
Chads Henry	Capt RN	2.548	
Chalmers William		14.429	
		14.437	
Chalmers Robert	Sir	18.268	
Chamberlayne Chas.	Adm	23.440	
Chambers W	Mr	11.494	
Chambers	Mr	12.432	son of Sir S Chambers
Chambers Samuel		15.258	
Chambers Thomas		22.137	
Champain Wm B	Capt RN	40.243	
Champion William		20.253	
Champion William B	Lt RN	31.440	

Chandler George		14.258	
Chantrell William	Lt RN	6.84	
Chapman P	Capt	7.92	
Chapman	Master	16.264	son of Lt Chapman RN
Chapman	Adm	20.423	
Chapman Daniel		27.87	
Chapman Samuel		27.506	
Chappe M		13.246	inventor of the Telegraph
Charles Hornsby	Lt RN	8.88	
Charles Thomas		21.438	
Charlotte John		16.349	
Charlotte Augusta	HRH Princess	38.420	
Charlton William	Lt	19.264	
Charlton William	Capt RN	24.439	
Charlton	R Adm	33.176	
Charnock John		17.440	
Charrier Jacques S		25.515	
Charrington	R Adm	9.251	
Cheddle John	Lt RM	33.512	
Cheeseman Richard		28.348	
Chester Wm	Lt RN	37.86	
Chesterman James		7.78	
Chilcot	Capt RN	9.166	
Child	Mr	10.175	
Child John George		25.352	
Child Smith	Adm	29.176	
Chitchagoff E'beth	Mrs	26.180	a daughter of Commissioner Proby RN
Chreshop Wm		37.264	
Christian	Lady	1.176	wife of Admiral Sir HC C., KB
Christian H C	Adm Sir	1.263	
Christie Robert		6.172	
Christiernin	Adm	2.83	Swedish Navy
Christopher Charles		21.342	
Christopher	Mrs	24.440	wife of Henry Christopher
Chubb Sarah	Mrs	26.440	
Chugg William		20.251	
Church	Miss	13.86	daughter of Capt Church RM
Church Henry		32.439	
Churchill Joseph D	Lt	25.88	
Claggett John		27.345	
Clark	Capt	7.180	of the Suffolk
Clark W	Mr	14.174	
Clark	Lt RM	16.176	
Clark John		27.264	
Clarke	Mrs	2.83	mother of Lt Clarke of the Argus, frigate
Clarke	Mrs	13.246	widow of Capt Peter C., RN
Clarke George	Capt RN	14.287	
		14.350	
Clarke	Lt RN	24.352	of the Crane
Clarke William		25.433	
Clarke William		29.348	landman of the Java
Clarke W		30.522	Capt of Rebecca, privateer
Clarke James Henry		35.516	
Clarke A	Doctor	40.500	

Claypitt	Mr	23.352	at Portsea
Clayton T W	Capt RN	16.88	
Clayton Joshua		20.419	
Cleather G	Mrs	1.176	
Cleather E	Capt RN	8.440	
Clements	Capt	1.176	
Clements W	Lt	12.255	
Clements	Mrs	21.352	widow of Capt Peter C., RN
Clerk John		27.438	
Clewlow J H		29.440	
Clifford John	Doctor	27.176	
Clitheroe Thomas		27.506	
Clitherow James	Lt RN	30.88	
Clowes	Mr	32.439	Purser of the North Star
Cobb Matthew		5.356	
Cobb	Lt RN	26.343	of the Castilian
		27.87	
Cobb James		39.498	
Cochrane	Lt	26.351	agent for transports, Halifax
Cochrane George		33.166	
Cock James	Capt	35.176	
Cockburne George	Lt RN	1.88	
Cockcraft	Mrs	27.264	wife of W Cockcraft
Cockerell	Mrs	1.348	widow of Samuel Cockerell, packet-boat commander, Harwich
Cocks	Mrs	31.512	widow of Wm Cocks
Codd G P R	Lt	32.340	of 85th Light Infantry
Codd S	Lt RN	34.352	
Codlin Richard		21.438	
Coffin J	Lt	22.176	
Coffinger John	Lt RN	34.440	
Coghill J	Sir	37.518	
Coglan Luke		16.349	
Coghlan John		25.434	
Cole	Mr	10.175	Mid of the Blenheim
Cole Martin	Commander	11.494	
Cole	Lt	12.511	
Cole John		19.176	
Cole John		22.137	
Coleman J G		23.352	
Coles David		24.504	
Colgrave	Capt RN	31.438	at Plymouth
Colleton John	Sir	6.172	
Collett	Mrs	17.440	widow of Pitt Collett HEIC
Colley Edward		27.439	
Collier George		16.79	
Collier James		19.515	
Collier	Lt	23.520	of the Achille
Collier James	Lt RN	26.87	
Collier	Mrs	26.87	widow of J Collier
Collier	Lt Col	31.512	
Collins John		7.78	
Collins Henry	Capt RN	7.180	
Collins	Lt Col RM	24.440	

Collins	Mr	24.516	Superintending Master at Plymouth
Collins Wm Martin	Lt RN	30.88	
Collins William		31.349	
Collingwood Cuthbert	V Adm Lord	23.350	
Collis Samuel	Reverend	25.513	
Collman	Mr	12.342	Purser of the Hippoenes
Colnet	Capt	16.264	late of the Glatton
Colnett	Mrs	25.176	wife of Capt Colnett HEIC
Colnett M	Mrs	39.423	sister of Capt Colnett RN
Columbine	Mrs	24.516	wife of Capt Columbine RN, governor of Sierra Leone
Columbine Edward H	Capt	26.88	
Columbine Edward H		36.174	son of previous entry?
Colville John	Lord	25.263	
Colwell Dennis		29.78	
Coming David		20.251	
Comyns Valence	Lt RN	24.87	
Confidine	Lt	9.423	
Conn	Capt RN	23.520	of the Swiftsure
Connell P		33.262	
Conner William		25.432	
Connolly Michael		29.241	
Conquer John		36.264	
Considine	Capt	18.240	of the 87th Regmt
Consolva Anthony		16.174	
Conway John		27.345	
Conyers Titus	Capt RM	25.352	
Cooban R B	Lt RN	25.176	
Cood Richard		24.176	
Cook Alexander	Capt	1.175	
Cook Thomas	Mr	1.175	
Cook James	Lt	3.516	
Cook John		25.164	
Cook Thomas		25.433	
Cook Thomas		6.406	
Cooke John		14.437	
Cooke	Lt RN	19.440	of the Minerva
Cooke W	Lt RN	36.440	
Cooksley	Mrs	24.264	wife of Capt Cooksley
Coombe Henry	Capt RN	5.544	
Coombe	Capt RN	21.176	of the Heureux
Coonber George		25.434	
Cooper R Palliser	R Adm	14.350	
Cooper William		17.347	
Cooper George		29.257	
Cooper T R		36.87	
Copes John		21.343	
Coppinger H S		6.516	
Corbet John Meek		26.88	
Corbett Robert	Capt	25.161	
		25.176	
Corbyn Edward		15.429	
Cordroy William		33.166	
Corfe Joseph		5.376	
Corlett John		29.258	

Corlyn Edmund		14.437	
Cormick William M'C		23.88	
Corner	Capt HEIC	40.243	
Cornet	Monsieur	5.361	of the French Navy
Cornish Samuel	Adm	35.352	
Cornish James	Capt RN	37.87	
Cornwallis James	Capt	1.174	
Cornwallis	the Hon Mrs	26.264	wife of the Bishop of Lichfield
Cosby Phillips	Adm	19.88	
Cotes James	Capt RN	7.532	
Cotgrave Isaac	Capt RN	31.512	
Cotton Charles	Adm Sir	27.176	
Cotterell William H		31.87	
Cottrell Frederick	Capt RN	25.264	
		25.515	
Cottrell John		29.176	
Couch	Capt	17.440	of the Epervier
Coulson Thomas jnr		30.360	
Countess George	R Adm	25.176	
Courcy de	Miss	13.86	daughter of the Hon. Capt de Courcy RN
Court Peter Van	Lt	18.348	
Court C	Capt	31.439	
Court W P Ache a	Sir	38.176	
Courtnell	Mrs	32.439	age 90 yrs, mother of W Courtnell
Coutee John		15.257	
Coutts	Mrs	14.350	widow of Capt Coutts RM
Coveney	Mr	6.260	Purser of the Mondovi
Covey		15.440	of the Venerable
Cowie Alexander		28.348	
Cowley John	Mr	18.268	
Cowpar Henry	Mr	25.176	
Cox John		6.406	AB on the La Pomone
Cox	Mr	12.511	
Cox Thomas		27.345	
Cox William		28.169	
Coxe Edward	Capt RM	36.440	
Cracraft	Capt RN	23.264	Commander of the Sea Fencibles on Sussex coast
		23.520	
Crandon Benjamin		22.137	
Crane John	Lt RN	3.240	
Crane	Mr	9.497	Mid, son of MasterAttendant of Dock-yard, Portsmouth
Crane	Mr	28.88	last First Master Attendant, Portsmouth
Cranmer Thomas		21.348	
Cranstoun	Mrs	21.87	widow of Capt C. RN
Crawford	Lt RN	21.88	
Crawford	Mr	24.515	master's mate of the Pearlen
Crawford Robert		31.257	
Crawley P A		31.425	
Crawley Samuel		31.425	
Crawley John	Capt RN	35.86	
Creed Mr		20.256	son of Mr Creed, Navy Agent
Crees		5.280	

Name	Rank	Ref	Note
Creighton	Mr	27.515	Purser of the Indian
Crese William		24.165	
Cresswell	Major RM	13.246	
Crew James		31.425	
Crews	Lt RN	25.264	
Crickitt John		26.264	
Crisp William		20.253	
Crispigny de	Capt	30.264	
		30.360	
Crispin Thomas		29.258	
Croad	Capt RM	6.516	
Croft John	Capt RN	20.80	
Crofton F J L	Lt	40.243	
Crofton Ellen S	Miss	40.243	an infant
Croker John		31.512	
Croker Walter		38.348	
Croll Robert		20.168	
Crookman Henry		21.347	
Crookshanks	Mr	12.166	Sgn of the Fort Diamond
Cropley	Lt	23.440	
Crosby Phillip		27.506	
Cross Samuel		21.438	
		21.520	
Crow Samuel	Lt RM	34.352	
Crowdery	Mr	36.87	Sgn attached to the African Expedition
Crymes John	Capt RN	36.264	
Cudlipp	Capt RN	14.174	
Cudlipp Charles		33.176	
Cullum John		36.518	
Culverhouse	Capt RN	21.352	and his wife
Cumberlege	Capt	13.246	his infant son
Cumby D P	Capt RN	32.176	
Cumby Ann	Mrs	33.176	
Cuming	Capt	14.511	of the Castle Eden, Indiaman
Cuming	Mrs	20.167	wife of Dr Ralph Cuming
Cuming Ralph	Doctor	20.168	
Cumming James	Adm	20.167	
Cundy Thomas		24.438	
Cunningham Alexander	Mr	1.446	
Cunningham	Mr	26.264	of the Foudroyant
Cunningham G	Lt RM	28.440	
Curling Robert		3.240	
Curry Robert	Capt RN	28.440	aged 80 years
Curtis Roger	RN	8.88	
Curtis Hyde	Capt RN	23.352	
Curtis Richard		25.434	
Curtis Thomas		29.78	
Curtis Roger	Adm Sir	36.440	
Curtis	Lady	37.352	widow of Admiral Sir Roger Curtis RN
Cuthbert James	Lt	23.440	
Cuthbertson R	Capt RM	15.87	
Cuyler	Lt	37.434	of the 30th Regmt
Dacres	V Adm	23.88	

Dadd Robert		37.264	
Dadd Stephen John	Mr	39.423	Surgeon RN
Daggon William		24.175	
Dalby Henry		25.264	
Daley Daniel	Lt RN	25.86	
Daley James		27.506	
Dalling Richard		20.419	
Dalmer H	Reverend	11.87	
Dalrymple James	Capt RN	9.423	
Dalrymple C	Mrs	20.424	
Dalton Thomas		40.73	
Damarell Henry		37.176	
Dalyell William C C	Lt RN	13.166	
Damerel	Mr	3.502	master of the Penelope
Danney (i) William		13.410	
Danney (ii) William		13.410	
Danvers	Capt RM	18.520	
		19.88	
Darby James		25.341	
Darley James		24.255	
Darling James	Capt RN	6.348	
Darouk Peter		21.347	
Dashwood	Miss	30.360	daughter of Capt Chas D., RN
Date F	Mrs	12.432	sister of Adm Jefferies
D'Auvergne Philip	V Adm	36.264	
Davers	Capt RN	11.87	late of the Active
Davey	Mr	18.520	of the Boreas
Davey Francis Surrage		25.433	
Davey John Hoam		28.161	
Davidson James		24.424	
Davidson William		28.434	
Davie	Capt-Lt RM	8.264	
Davie John		37.168	
Davies J	Lt	12.431	
Davies Charles		22.251	
Davies	Mrs	28.263	wife of W A Davies
Davis Joseph		3.516	
Davis	Reverend	5.96	Chaplain of the Q. Charlotte on the Glorious 1st June
Davis Morgan		6.61	
Davis Owen	Mr	13.86	chart maker
Davis John		19.259	
Davis	Lt RN	24.352	on passage from India
Davis Jacob		26.515	
Davis Richard	Lt RN	30.522	
Davis J H		32.264	
Davis William		32.435	
Davis	Mrs	35.264	at Gosport
Davis	Lt RN	39.176	
Daw Thomas		33.166	
Dawal John		12.413	
Dawes	Lt	19.88	agent for transports
Dawson Jos		19.259	
Dawson John		25.434	
Dawson Henry	Capt RN	27.351	
Dawson Hutton	Capt RN	29.440	

Day	Mr	13.335	Gunner of the Terror
Day W	Capt RN	15.352	
Deacon	Capt RN	29.264	at Montrose, Scotland
Dean J E		24.439	
Dean Henry		32.511	
Deane Phillip	Capt	5.376	
Deane Thomas		25.434	
Deans	Capt	19.176	of the Prince of Wales packet
Deans Robert	Adm	33.88	
Dear Thomas		35.86	
De Busk W	Lt RN	10.350	
De Courcy Michael	Capt Hon	30.176	
Dedel	Adm	4.444	of the Dutch Marine
Delafons	Capt	13.335	of the Dasher
Delafons John		32.439	
Delafons	Mrs	35.352	at Tamerton, Devon
Delanoe George A		7.180	RN
De Launois	Ensign	6.501	
Denne	Lt RM	20.80	
Dent Digby	Capt RN	1.88	
Dent Digby	R Adm Sir	37.352	
Derbyshire William		32.170	
Dermon John		24.165	
Desborough	Mrs	8.176	wife of Col D., RM
Despard John		6.348	
De Vaumorel	Capt	37.434	of the 30th Regmt
Dewar James		28.264	
De Winter	Adm	28.88	
Dewsnap Martha	Miss	19.176	
Dewsnap Joseph	Lt RN	20.256	infant son of
Dewsnap Ann	Miss	27.176	
Dewsnap Rebecca	Miss	27.176	
Dewsnap Joseph		28.264	
Dewson	Mr	27.440	of Portsea
Dick	Mrs	31.262	mother of Capt Dick RN
Dickins George	Capt RN	33.352	
Dickins Francis G	Capt RN	39.264	
Dickinson William		19.88	aged 101 years
Dickinson	Mrs	26.351	wife of Major D. RM
Dickinson F	Capt RN	27.515	
Dickinson Charles		33.172	
Dickinson James	Capt RN	33.512	of the Penguin
Dickson	Mrs	1.262	wife of Admiral A Dickson
Dickson William	Adm	9.497	
Dickson Archibald	Adm Sir	9.498	
Dickson John	General	35.440	
Digby Charles	Rev Hon	26.351	
Digby Richard	Adm	31.262	
Dinan J Bartholomew		29.175	
Dinnacombe James		30.248	
Dirks John		29.258	
Dixon George		7.85	
Dixon Charles	Capt	11.494	
Dixon J W T	Capt	11.494	
Dixon	Mrs	23.352	wife of R Admiral Dixon
Dobie Adam D		4.528	

Dobree Daniel E		16.88	
Dobree	Capt RN	32.352	at Ramsbury, Wilts
		33.88	
Dobree R	Capt RN	39.264	
Dobson	Lt RN	15.176	
Dobson Edward		33.171	
Dod Michael	Capt RN	32.439	
Dod Edmund	R Adm	35.87	
Dodd Charlotte	Mrs	20.494	
Dodgson Percy C	Lt RN	17.352	
Dods	Mrs	26.180	wife of Dr Dods of Haslar Hosp
Doel John		29.348	
Doham	Lt	6.435	
Doig W	Capt	24.439	
Domett	Lt	11.494	
Domville	Mr	13.165	son of C Domville of Powick
Donaldson Hugh	Capt	12.255	
Donaldson James		13.157	
Donelan George		14.258	
Donnellan John M	Lt RN	36.87	
Donnelly Anne	Mrs	23.352	
Donnithorne Thomas	Capt RN	24.515	
		26.352	
Donolly Patrick		25.434	
Donvill		12.511	
Doris Thomas		32.435	
Douglas	Lady	4.348	widow of Sir Charles
Douglas James	Lt RN	13.246	
Douglas William H	V Adm Sir	21.520	
Douglas J L	Adm	24.440	
		24.516	
Douglas Sarah L	Miss	25.264	
Douglas Roddam	Capt RN	30.360	
Douglas T W	Lt	30.522	
Douglas John	Major Gen Sir	31.262	
Douglas Thomas		31.426	
Douglas Francis		37.176	
Douglas	Capt	37.256	of the 11th Regmt
Douglas Frances	Rt Hon Lady	37.352	
Douglas Billy	Adm	38.511	
Douglas G R	Capt RN	39.87	
Douglas John	Commodore	40.84	Commander RN in service of the King of Portugal
Douty	Mr	36.264	aged 84 years, at Plymouth
Dover James	Lt	32.176	
Dowdeswell Thomas		26.440	
Dowers William	Capt RN	37.264	
Downes Peter	Mr	1.174	
Downey Thomas		36.174	
Downie George	Capt RN	32.439	
		33.257	
Doyle John		24.168	
Drake Thomas		24.88	
Drake William		24.88	
Drane	Lt RN	23.352	at Exmouth
Draper James		26.343	

Draper John	Capt RN	29.264	
Dredge John		28.88	
		28.264	repeat of above
Dreminsky Charles		30.259	
Drew	Capt RN	11.168	
Drew (i) J	Lt RN	12.342	at Stokaton, nr Saltash
		12.432	
Drew (ii) J	Lt	12.342	nephew of Capt Drew of the
		12.432	Cerebus
Drew (iii) J	Capt	12.342	of the Cerebus
		12.432	
Drew (iv) J	Capt	12.342	of the de Braak
		12.432	
Drew John		15.121	
Driffield	Lt Col RM	5.376	son-in-law of Capt Wm Bligh
Driscole James		15.257	
Drummond C		23.352	of the HEIC
Drummond Robert	Lt RN	25.515	
Drury	Lt RN	21.87	of the Modeste
Drury William O'B	V Adm	26.179	
Drury	Miss	31.88	sister of the late Admiral Drury
Ducie Francis R M	Capt RN, Lord	20.256	
Duckworth John T	Adm Sir	28.262	
Dudley William		25.432	
Duer John	Capt RN	32.440	
Duff George	Capt RN	14.429	
		14.437	
Duff Alexander		14.429	
		14.437	
Duff James	Capt RM	32.264	
Dufferin & Claneboye	Baroness	17.176	
Duggan James		27.507	
Duguet	Monsieur	5.360	of the French Navy
Duke William	Lt RN	17.164	
Dumaresq Thomas	Adm	8.87	
Dumaresq	Capt RN	30.522	
Duncan Alexander	Capt Hon	9.165	of the Guards
Duncan	Adm Lord	12.165	
Duncan Thomas		13.157	
Duncan Alexander		22.504	
Duncan William		25.433	
Dundas Charles	Mrs	23.175	sister to Lord Melville
Dundas	R Adm	25.515	
Dundas George	R Adm	32.439	
Dunlop John	Capt	24.516	
Dunn John		29.348	supernumerary of the Java
Dunn R D	Capt RN	29.512	
Dunn John		30.84	captain's clerk of Shannon
Dunstell	Mr	18.520	of the Boreas
Dunsterville B	Lt RN	6.348	
Duree H A	Capt RM	37.86	
Durell Thomas	Capt	11.494	
Durell T P	Capt	11.494	
Durell	Mrs	33.512	wife of Capt Thomas Phillip
			Durell RN
Durham	Lt RN	29.264	of the Neptune, tender

Duttan Charles		31.426	
Duvan	Mr	19.176	Gunner of the Royal Charlotte
Dyer R		22.176	
Dyer Ann	Mrs	30.360	
Dyer George	Major Gen RM	38.176	
Dyer J W	Lt RN	39.87	
Dyneley	Capt	19.264	of the Duke of Montrose
Eagersfield	Mr	19.176	of the Sparkler
Eaglestone	Capt RN	28.352	of the Procris
Ealey James		28.162	
Earle	Mrs	26.264	wife of Arthur Earle
Eastman J E	Lt	24.176	
Easton	Lt RN	23.520	
Eaud John	Mr	1.348	
Eddington	Miss	37.440	at Portsea
Edgar	Capt RA	25.264	
Edgar George	Lt RN	34.512	
Edgar Alexander	R Adm	37.176	aged 80 years
Edgecombe	Mrs	27.87	mother of Fred. E.
Edgecombe John	Capt	27.515	sailed with Capt Cook
Edgcumb Richard		9.166	
Edgecumbe	Miss	26.515	sister of Capt E.
Edwards	Mrs	3.240	wife of Capt Edwards
Edwards Thomas		14.428	
Edwards	Mrs	25.352	widow of Capt Edwards RN, of Nanoron, Caerns
Edwards Rice V	Capt RN	26.351	
Edwards George		29.258	
Edwards John B	Capt RN	29.440	
Edwards John		33.340	
Edwards Edward	Adm	33.512	
Egerton John		31.439	
Eglington Anthony		19.264	of the HEIC
Elers	Lt RN	33.264	at Stoke, nr Plymouth
Ellery William		30.507	
Elliot John	Adm	20.336	
Elliott	Mr	7.180	Mid on the Severn
Elliott	Lt RM	13.246	
Elliott James		20.418	
Elliott	Lt	23.264	of the Sceptre
Elliott	Mrs	26.515	mother of Sgt Major Holder RM
Elliott William	Hon	26.515	
Elliott W	Capt	27.515	infant son of
Elliott	Capt	31.348	of the Martial
Ellis Charles	the Hon Mrs	9.166	
Ellis	Mrs	12.166	wife of Capt Ellis RN, daughter of Capt Cole
Ellis Henry		15.264	
Ellis Daniel		20.253	
Ellis John		21.347	
Ellis Frederick	Lt RN	23.440	
Ellison Cuthbert W	Lt RN	5.187	
Ellison Dorothy	Miss	23.352	3rd daughter of Capt Joseph E., RN. See also Mrs Basden
Ellison Charles P H	Lt RN	35.264	

Ellison Joseph	Capt RN	36.352	
Ellison William	Capt RN	37.176	
Ellitson	Capt RN	40.244	
Elphinstone John	Capt RN	7.180	
Elphinstone	Mr	7.452	Sgn of the Weazle
Elphinstone Clementina	Lady Dowager	1.262	
Emerson Benjamin		31.175	
Emondson William (or Arthur)		33.165/6	
Empson John Masters		8.264	
England Jos	Capt RN	39.176	
English	Mr	24.515	master's mate of the Pearlen
Enlay Daniel		25.164	
Ennis	Mrs	28.439	widow of Rev E M Ennis
Epworth	R Adm	11.263	
Errington Thomas	Lt RN	22.352	
Esdale Samuel		37.168	
Eshelby Thomas	Mr	25.176	the Sgn who amputated Lord Nelson's arm
Esplin John	Capt HEIC	2.263	
Essington Wm	V Adm Sir	36.87	
Etty William	Mr	21.520	
Eunson John	Capt	24.439	
Evans William		4.444	
Evans	Lt	11.494	
Evans John		22.259	
Evans George	Mr	24.175	
Evans William		27.506	
Evans John		32.435	
Evans John	Capt	35.352	at Hoxton
Everard	Capt	32.352	of the Wasp
		34.440	
Evertz C J		17.170	
Eves Francis Walwin		10.263	
Eyres James	Mr	25.88	
Fabian Robert		37.175	
Fagan James		29.348	
Fahie Eliza	Mrs	38.88	
Fair William		33.171	
Fair J		33.262	
Fairfax Margaret	Miss	14.262	
Fairfax William G	V Adm Sir	30.448	
Falconer John		21.438	
Falkland	Rt Hon Lord Viscount	21.264	
Fallon	Lt	18.240	of 38th Regmt
Fane Nevill		19.88	
Fanshawe R	Capt RN	12.165	
Farley William		13.410	
Farlow John		38.176	
Farrer Henry		4.256	HEIC
Farquhar Thomas	Doctor	40.332	
Farquarhson James R	Capt RN	21.176	
Farquharson R S	Lt RN	25.87	

Farquharson	Mrs	28.440	widow of Dr Farquharson
Farr William		22.352	MD
Farrington	Mr	24.440	Sgn of the Narcissus
Farthing Thomas		23.165	
Faulkner	Mrs	24.175	widow of Adm Faulkner
		24.440	
Faulknor Jonathan	R Adm	21.88	
Fawkes William		21.260	
Fead Robert	Major RA	2.644	
Fearon Charles		24.515	
Feeland John		25.164	
Felix Tomaso		24.504	
Fenalson Andrew		31.425	
Fenlayson Henry		13.410	
Fennel G	Lt	14.262	
Fennell John		25.87	
Ferguson Alexander		3.315	
Ferguson Adam	Capt RM	14.174	
Ferguson	Asst Sgn	18.240	of the 88th Regmt
Ferguson P	Capt HEIC	24.515	
Ferguson John		25.164	
Ferguson Gilbert		26.179	
Ferguson	Mrs	31.352	wife of Capt George Ferguson
		31.512	
Fernyhough	Lt RM	10.517	
Fernynough	Lt	14.512	of the Donnegal
Ferrell Lawrence		27.506	
Ferri William	Capt RN	35.440	
Ferris Solomon	Capt RN	10.87	
Festing H	Capt RN	18.174	
Fielding	Lt RN	23.88	of the Helder
Fielding	Mrs	33.352	widow of the late Capt Charles Fielding RN
Finisker Christopher		21.438	
Finlayson	Mrs	34.352	mother of Lt F. RN
Finlesson Alexander		29.258	
Finnis Robert	Capt RN	31.253	
Finucane Patrick		24.507	
Firmidge	Lt	12.511	of the Diana
Firth William		29.78	
Fitgerald John		7.78	
Fitzgerald	Capt RM	11.494	
Fitzgerald James		27.506	
Fitzhugh H	Mr	19.421	
Fitzmaurice Thomas	Doctor	37.88	
Fitzpatrick John		40.74	
Fitzroy Augustus	Lord	6.348	
Fleetwood	Lt	25.440	agent for transports, Jersey
Fleming George F		32.440	
Fleylen Henry van		15.434	
Flinders Matthew	Capt	32.88	
Flinn Patrick		27.511	
Flintoft William		21.347	
		21.352	
Flynn	Lt RN	24.88	
Folds T J	Lt RN	40.244	

Foote Charles	Capt RN	27.351	
Foote Catherine	Miss	29.440	
Foote Mary	Mrs	37.86	
Forbes John		3.516	
Forbes George	Lt RN	36.518	
Forbitt Alexander		29.352	
Ford I B		24.175	
Ford E		24.440	
Ford Dennis		28.162	
Ford William		31.172	
Foreman H	Asst Sgn	18.437	
Forfar William		9.165	
Forode James		14.167	
Forrest Austen	Capt	28.440	
Forrester	Mrs	1.348	widow of Rev Dr Forrester, surviving sister of Adm Sir John Moore
Forrester David		7.350	
Forster Jean R	Mr	1.176	
Forster	Lt Col RM	6.516	
Forster William		14.429	
		14.438	
Forster	Lt	14.512	of the Colossus
Forster R D	Capt RM	29.264	
Forten	Mr	36.264	at Torpoint, Master RN
Fortescue John	Capt RN	20.168	
Forth	Mrs	37.86	wife of John Forth
Foster William	Lt RN	9.81	of West End nr S'hmptn
Foster William	Lt RN	9.165	no details
Foster Stephen	Capt RN	19.352	
Foster William		30.248	seaman of the Isabella
Foster William		31.426	landman on the Hannibel
Fothergill William	Capt RN	38.176	
Foulks John D		29.440	
Foulkes Joseph		21.344	
Fowers John		14.258	
Fowke Thomas T	Major	9.423	
Fowke	Capt RN	27.439	his eldest son
Fowler Frederic T	Lt RM	24.264	
Fowler	Mrs	36.264	wife of Capt Fowler RN
Fox James		28.162	
Fox J A		28.348	
Fox George		31.257	
Foxton	Mr	38.348	Master RN, of the Hyaena
Fraine	Capt RN	7.364	
Frampton Charles		2.263	
Francillon	Mr	39.498	Mid of the Rochfort
Francis John		17.343	
Francis Robert		29.258	
Francisco Anthony		29.258	
Franckland William		36.87	
Frankland Harriet	Miss	19.87	
Frankland	Dowager Lady	19.352	widow of Adm Sir T Frankland, mother of Sir T Frankland
Frankland	Mr	25.87	of the Hussar
		25.264	

Fraser John	Lt RN	29.88	
Frazer Henry T	Capt RN	36.264	
Frazer	Mrs	37.88	wife of Lt Col Frazer RM
Frederick Thomas L	R Adm	2.548	
		3.80	
Freeman Edward		22.251	of the Minotaur
Freeman Edward		23.170	of the Blonde
Freeman	Mid	23.352	of the Scipion
Freeman	Mr	24.515	B'swain of the Pearlen
Freers Robert		18.348	
Frehling Joseph		22.251	
Freke William		23.338	
French Arthur	Mr	19.515	
Friar Robert		32.435	
Froud A		12.166	Surgeon
Froud P	Lt RN	12.166	
Fuller James		2.82	at Sheerness
Fuller James		24.165	marine on the Spartan
Fulton Robert		33.512	
Furbor Thomas		13.85	
Furmidge	Lt	13.246	of the Diana
Furnall Harry	Capt RN	14.352	
Furness	Lt RN	15.352	of the Illustrious
Furneval William	Lt RN	24.87	
Gadsby Edward		14.258	
Gahan Daniel	Major	21.352	
Galpine Thomas		16.176	
Gamage Richard S	Lt RN	28.501	
		29.25	
Gambier Samuel		29.440	
Gamble Richard	Capt	1.262	
Garden James	Lt	31.253	Ryl Newfoundland Regmt
Gardiner Frederick		26.87	
Gardner	Mr	6.172	Purser of the Fox
Gardner John		15.257	
Gardner George		19.440	
Gardner	Adm Lord	21.87	
Gardner	Lady	25.352	
Gardner Thomas		29.258	
Gardner Francis G	Capt RM	30.522	
Gardner H S	Lt RN	33.440	of the Phoebe
Gardner	V Adm Lord	35.87	
Gardner Valentine		35.176	
Gardner John	Lt RN	36.87	
Garland John	Lt RN	31.253	
Garnier J	Capt	7.92	
Garnier Elizabeth	Lady	30.88	
Garrett	Mrs	28.264	wife of Capt H Garrett
Garthshore	Mrs	10.175	wife of William G., MP
Gascoigne William		29.348	
Gascoyne	Mr	13.504	master of the Beaulieu
Gasson James		30.235	
Gatehouse	Lt RN	26.440	
Gatt James		22.162	
Gavanough Andrew		30.507	

Gay Charles		24.168	
Gayler	Lt RN	10.517	
Geall Ebenezer	Lt RN	14.437	
Gearman Thomas		32.163	
Geary Thomas	Capt RN	13.166	
		13.246	
Geddies James		4.528	
Gell John		2.247	
Gell John	Adm	16.515	
Gellie Lewis		28.264	aged 98 years
George Rupert		18.520	
George John		25.434	
George Samuel Hood		29.512	
German Thomas		30.85	
Gerond G B Z		17.170	
Ghiogonio George		27.506	
Gibbes Anthony	Capt RN	32.439	
Gibbings Richard		20.418	
		20.424	
Gibbons W		6.147	
Gibbs Thomas		1.263	
Gibbs William		19.342	
Gibbs Thomas	Lt	24.515	
Gibbs	Mrs	36.518	daughter of Adm Sir William Rowley RN
Gibson Thomas		22.504	
Gibson John		25.352	
Gibson Robert	Lt RN	36.87	
Gidney	Lt RM	25.87	
Gifferena G		28.88	
Gilbert Michael	Mr	1.176	
Gilbert Thomas	Lt RN	9.166	
Gilbert Frances	Miss	26.179	
Gilbert G		30.85	
Gilbert William		30.176	
Gilchrist Mary	Mrs	1.176	
Gilchrist Neil		30.85	
Giles James		16.349	
Gill	Mr	21.176	Sgn of the Royals
Gill Jas	Lt RN	26.179	
Gill	Mr	33.352	father of Capt C Gill
Gillespie Thomas	Lt RN	6.516	
Gillespie	Mr	16.264	Sgn of the Morne Fortunee
Gillford John		16.349	
Gillies William		12.166	
Gilliland Brice	Lt RN	14.429	
		14.437	
Glen John		34.88	
Glennie George Ross		36.352	
Glover	Lt RM	6.435	
Glynn	Mrs	28.513	wife of Capt Glynn RN
Goddard William		14.258	
Goddard William		26.179	
Goddard W	Mr	39.88	father of Thos Goddard, Purser of the Royal George, yacht
Godfrey William B		27.87	

Name	Rank/Title	Ref	Note
Godsalve G	Mrs	12.511	
Godwin James	Lt RN	27.88	
Gooch Samuel	Lt	11.494	
Goodall Samuel G	Adm	5.375	
		5.464	
Goode Thomas		25.87	
Goode Pittman	Mrs	28.263	
Gooding Nathaniel	Capt RN	26.88	
Goodman John		2.247	
Goodman R		26.179	
Goodridge	Lt RN	1.261	Commander of the Dispatch, schooner
Goodson Samuel	Lt RN	6.348	
Goodwin	Lt RN	23.88	of the Pickle
Gordon John	Lt	16.264	
Gordon Charles		20.418	
Gordon	Miss	25.352	niece of Adm Ferguson
Gordon	Mrs	27.440	surviving sister of the late Capt James Bremner RN
Gordon John	Lt RN	31.262	
Gordon	Lt RN	33.264	at Plymouth Hospital
Gordon Charles F		38.88	
Gore William		6.157	
Gore William	Mid	6.172	of the Medusa
		6.260	
Gore J	the Hon	27.439	
Gore Arthur	Brig Gen	31.439	of 33rd Regmt of Foot
Gore Harriet S	Miss	37.176	
Gosselin Sarah	Mrs	34.512	
Gostling Francis	Lt RN	31.512	
Gough David		26.433	
Gould	Mr	24.175	Surgeon RN
Gould Isaac		28.166	
Gould	Mrs	29.512	at Portsea
Gourley Samuel	Capt	24.87	
Gower Leveson	the Hon Mrs	6.84	
Gower Augustus L	Capt RN	8.352	
Gower	Major RM	8.440	brother of Sir Erasmus Gower
Gower Erasmus	Adm Sir	32.176	conflicting dates of death
Graeme Alexander	Adm	40.244	
Grafton	Duke of	25.264	
Gragg John		25.434	
Graham Joseph		22.137	AB on the Implacable
Graham Joseph		32.511	shipbuilder of Harwich
Grahme William	Capt	4.444	
Grainger R G	Lt RM	29.258	
		29.264	
Grant	Lt	5.356	of the Rifle Corps
Grant T		8.440	
Grant Duncan		17.520	
Grant Samuel	Lt RN	38.88	
Grave William		6.147	
Graves William		5.544	elder brother of Adm Lord Graves
Graves	Lord	7.180	
Graves Samuel	R Adm	8.520	

Name		Rank/Title	Ref	Note
Graves	John		15.258	
Graves		Mrs	20.493	widow of R Adm Graves
Graves		Miss	23.352	daughter of Adm Graves
Graves		R Adm	25.513	
Graves		Lady	35.176	wid of Adm Sir Thos Graves
Gray	George	Lt	5.356	
Gray	John		6.61	
Gray	Allan		12.255	
Gray	William		23.352	
Gray	David	Lt RM	30.360	
Gray		Mr	31.352	of Portsmouth Dockyard
Gray	Walter		36.518	
Greaves	Jacob		26.83	
Greaves	Thomas	Adm Sir	31.352	
Green	Y	Lt RN	14.86	
Green	Robert	Lt RM	14.429	
			14.437	
Green	James		20.494	RM
Green	Charles		24.168	
Green	Henry		24.516	
Green	William	Capt RN	25.86	
Green	Thomas		27.506	
Green	G	Lt	33.88	late of the Steady
Greenway		Mrs	18.85	nee Maypoweder, wife of Lt G.
Greenway	Charles		31.257	
Greetham	C	Mr	24.88	
Gregory	George		11.175	age 109 years. Last of the crew of Anson's Centurion
Gregory		Lt	18.520	of the Maida
Gregory		Mrs	25.176	widow of Capt G. RN
Gregory	G	R Adm	31.176	
Greig	J S		13.166	
Greig	S		18.347	
Greig	James		29.258	
Greig	David		40.74	
Grey	Henry	Hon	1.348	
Grey		Rt Hon Earl	18.437	
Grey	James		26.83	
Grey	Charlotte	Miss	31.512	
Grey	William		33.176	3rd son of Earl Grey
Gribble	John		31.257	
Grier	Thomas		14.429	
			14.437	
Grierson		Lt RN	20.167	of the Melampus
Griffith	John	Lt RN	10.263	
Griffith	William		15.434	
Griffith	Susannah	Mrs	32.440	
Griffith		Mrs	33.88	wife of Capt John G. RN
Griffiths			16.439	Coxswain
Griffiths	Patrick		26.433	
Griffiths	Thos H	Lt RM	27.506	
Griffiths	George		28.348	
Griffiths	Thomas		32.170	
Grigg	John		25.164	
Grikand		Mr	13.335	RM
Grindall		Lt	9.251	of the Castor

Grindall Ed		27.87	
Grindall F H	Lt RN	27.515	
Grouville Lewis		20.251	
Grove T S	Capt RN	32.439	
Grueber Henry	Capt HEIC	21.520	
Grumby Richard		23.165	
Grumley	Mrs	32.511	mother of Capt G. RN
Guest Thomas		26.433	
Gundy William		15.434	
Gunhouse	Mrs	20.168	widow of Capt Ricard G.
Gunn Alexander		24.424	
Gunn W		33.257	
Guy H	Mrs	25.88	
Haddaway John	Lt RN	14.174	
Haddock John		16.439	
Haddon B F	Lt RN	13.165	
Haggett	Mrs	25.87	wife of Rev Dr Haggett
Hair	Lt RM	6.516	
Hake John		28.162	
Halbed M J R		27.438	of the HEIC
Hale Cecil		5.280	RN
Hale B	Capt	7.92	
Hales Samuel	Lt Sir	13.85	
		13.165	
Halfpenny William		23.88	
Halkett	Mrs	31.439	wife of R Adm Halkett
Halkett William	Capt HEIC	40.243	
Hall John	Capt HEIC	4.444	
Hall Charles F		6.435	
Hall E	Mrs	13.86	mother of Rev J Hall chaplain of Haslar Hospital
Hall	Capt	15.264	aged 107, Sgn's-mate on the Centurion under Anson
Hall	Lt	18.240	of the 88th Regmt
Hall John		21.176	
Hall	Miss	23.520	daughter of Adm Hall
Hall J	Capt	24.176	
Hall William		29.258	
Hall John S	V Adm	31.176	
Hall George		32.435	
Hall Robert	Capt Sir	39.343	
Hallam John	Capt RN	4.528	
Hallibenton John	Doctor	20.168	
Halliday	Mrs	37.87	wife of Capt Mich. H., RN
Hallowell Benjamin		2.172	
Hallum Thomas	R Adm	11.344	
Hallum Edward	Lt	11.494	
Halsted	Mrs	16.176	widow of Capt H. RN, mother of Capt W H. of the Namur
Hamilton	Lt	18.240	of the 6th Dragoon Gds
Hamilton	Lt RN	21.352	of the Unicorn
Hamilton	Mr	28.87	Asst Sgn, the President
Hamilton James		30.80	
Hamilton D S	Capt	32.340	of 85th Light Infantry
Hamilton T	V Adm RN	34.88	

Hammick John L	Lt RN	24.263	
Hammond James		13.410	
Hammond Charles	Mr	23.520	Purser of the Africaine
Hammond Charles	Mr	25.88	shipping agent at Deal
Hammond William		29.258	
Hammond Thomas		29.348	
Hamond	Miss	15.352	sister of Sir Andrew S Hamond
Hancock	Mr	22.88	of the Statira
Hancock William	Lt RN	35.352	
Hancorn	Lt RM	24.439	
Hancorne	Lt	12.255	ex Portuguese service
Handley Charles P		4.348	
Hankin Thomas		24.175	
Hanmer Ann E	Miss	14.512	
Hanmond T		38.511	
Hannaford H	Mr	16.440	
Hannam	Lt	12.166	of the Alligator
Hansell Joseph		24.439	
Hansford	Mrs	9.498	widow of Capt Hansford RN
Hansford	Mr	28.263	master plumber, Portsmouth Dockyard
Hansworth Cornelius		25.432	
Hanwell	Mr	36.259	Mid on the Leander
Happer Samuel		29.175	
Hardacre Octavia A	Miss	19.176	
Hardacre Helen	Mrs	20.256	and her infant child
Hardacre Helen	Mrs	26.88	
Hardacre Henry T	Master	26.88	
Hardacre Helen H	Miss	26.88	
Hardacre Octavia H	Miss	26.88	
Hardcastle Edward		3.80	
Hardinge G N	Capt RN	20.145	of the St Fiorenzo
		20.483	
Hardingham J D		24.515	
Hardick Chapman		31.257	
Hardy	Lady	5.188	widow of Sir C Hardy
Hardy	Miss	15.176	eldest dau of Adm Sir C Hardy
Hardy Alexander		25.433	
Hardy John		27.440	
Hardy Temple	Capt	31.352	
Hardy Andrew	Lt RN	35.264	
Hardy	Mrs	40.243	wife of Mr Hardy, Purser RN
Hardyman J	Miss	13.246	
Hardyman	Lt Col	28.176	of H. M. Ceylon Regmt
Hardyman	Capt	32.264	father of Capt Lucius H. RN
Hare	Capt	6.516	
Hare	Lt	28.264	of the Fervent
Harford Charles	Capt RN	20.336	
Hargrave	Capt	31.352	of the Teazer
Harker George		25.434	
Harland	Dowager Lady	13.166	widow of Adm Sir R H.
Harral	Mrs	25.86	sister of John Masters Empson (see Vol 8 p264)
Harries	Lt	19.87	of the Anson
Harrington	Lt RN	28.88	of the Ocean
Harriot James E	Mr	1.176	

Name	Title	Ref	Note
Harriott John		37.87	
Harris	Mr	13.246	Sgn of the Diana
Harris Eliza	Mrs	24.176	
Harris Edwin C	Lt RN	35.516	
Harris	Mrs	36.174	widow of Charles H.
Harris John		36.440	
Harrison	Lt RN	19.352	agent for transports
Harrison Jacob		20.419	
Harrison Thomas		22.505	
Harrogan David		29.348	
Hart William		17.343	
Hart P	Mr	23.88	
Hart G	R Adm	27.440	
Hart	Lt	30.264	of the Venus
Hart	Mrs	33.352	widow of Adm Hart
Hartley Louisa	Lady	26.351	
Hartwell John	Mr	5.188	
Hartwell	Lady	21.520	wife of Capt Sir Francis H.
Hartwell Francis		24.439	
Harvey	Lt	20.168	of the Superb
Harvey Henry	Adm Sir	25.86	
Harvey Robert		27.87	
Harvey Samuel		27.87	
Harvey Samuel		30.176	
Harvey James W	Capt RN	35.352	
Harvey Richard		37.264	
Harvey Judith	Mrs	38.264	
Harwood Earle	Capt RN	26.180	
Hassel	Mr	39.264	of the Tiber
Haswell Margaret	Mrs	21.520	
Haswell John	Capt RN	26.180	
Hatton George B	Lt RN	27.176	
Hatton E Finch	Lt RN	30.264	
Hawden	Mr	6.348	Master Porter, Portsmouth Dockyard
Hawford W	Lt RN	17.440	
Hawker T	Capt RN	18.438	
Hawkes	Lt	18.520	of the Boreas
Hawkes Richard	Lt	24.176	
Hawkes	Mrs	30.264	wife of E Hawkes
Hawkey Joseph	Lt RN	22.137	
		22.176	
Hawkins James		25.434	
Hawkins	Mrs	29.440	wife of Lt Hawkins RM
Hawkins John		36.258	
Hawksford James		20.250	
Hawse John		31.257	
Hay Alexander		26.261	
		26.439	
Hay Thomas		27.264	
Hayes Samuel		5.360	
Hayes Charles		25.432	
Hayes T		26.351	
Hayes John		29.258	
Haygarth W	Lt RN	23.352	Governor of the Naval Knights of Windsor

Hayley	Lt	6.435	
Hayman Charles	Lt	12.432	
Hayman John		17.176	
Hayne Carle		31.257	
Hayter Joseph		33.352	
Heacock R	Lt	28.88	
Heath	R Adm	34.88	
Heawood	Mr	24.175	Sgn of the Surinam
Hector	Comte d'	20.168	
Hector William	Mr	39.423	
Hedley John		13.165	
Heigham George	Lt RN	40.74	
Helpman	Mr	16.169	master's mate of the Conqueror
Helpman P	Lt	17.264	
Helpman	Lt RN	33.512	of the Fairy
Hemphill	Mr	16.264	former Purser of the Donnegal
Hemsworth Sarah	Mrs	27.515	
Henderson Thomas		7.364	
Henderson John		25.87	
Hendrickson John		26.433	
Hendrie	Capt RN	26.178	of the Star
Henly	Lt RN	26.178	of the Charybdis
Henslow	Lady	9.423	wife of Sir John Henslow
Henslow John	Sir	34.440	aged 85 years
Heppenstall	Capt RN	22.352	of the Kingfisher
Herbert	Capt RN, Hon	20.256	
Heron	Mr	13.423	Purser of the Hibernia
Herring Samuel		6.406	
Herring	Capt RN	11.175	of the Shark
Hewitt John		9.423	
Hewitt	Lt	19.88	
Hext	Lt	30.448	of the Marlborough
Heydon William		30.170	
Heywood	Mrs	35.86	wife of Capt Edmund Heywood
Hichans William		29.348	
Hickman	Lt RN	2.548	
Hicks	R Adm	5.464	
Hicks Henry		14.174	
Hicks	Capt	22.520	
Hicks	Lt RM	36.87	
Hicks	Mrs	38.348	widow of Admiral Hicks
Higgins Charles	Lt RN	19.264	
Higginson Elisha		22.157	
Hill	Lt RN	2.82	
Hill J		2.83	
Hill Richard	Capt RN	2.263	
Hill	Mrs	4.256	wife of Capt H Hill RN
Hill	Mr	9.81	Boatswain of the Chichester
Hill Thomas		14.258	
Hill	Mrs	17.440	widow of Adm Hill
Hill	Lt Col	26.87	of the 10th Foot, brother of Capt Hill of the Naiad
Hill Robert		27.345	
Hill Joseph		28.166	
Hill John		29.78	
Hill Charles	Lt RN	31.87	

Name	Title	Ref	Notes
Hill Sarah	Mrs	31.175	
Hill	Lt RM	35.264	at Plymouth Dock
Hiller Peter		9.251	
Hillier William		7.78	
Hills	Capt RN	11.344	
Hills	Capt	12.166	Commander of the Renard
Hills James	Capt RN	31.511	
Hinget G H V A		17.170	
Hinton John		30.259	
Hinton	Capt RN	32.440	at Chatham
Hire George	Lt	11.494	
Hitchins John		21.260	
Hitchins C B		27.88	
Hoare George		5.356	
Hobart Charles	Capt RN	30.176	
Hodge William		29.78	
Hodges M	Mrs	20.336	widow of Capt J Hodges
Hogan John		33.171	
Holland Edmund B		12.255	
Holland	Mr	28.440	of the Bucephalus
Holles	Miss	39.423	sister of Capt R P Holles RN
Hollis Robert		15.257	
Holloway	Mr	8.352	son of Adm John H.
Holmes	Lt	11.494	
Holmes Samuel	Lt RN	21.520	
Holmes James		29.78	
Holstein	Capt	25.346	Danish national
Holtaway William	Capt RM	32.161	
		32.163	
Home Roddam		5.187	
Home William		6.260	
Home George	V Adm Sir	9.423	
Home	Miss	10.263	eldest daughter of V Admiral Sir George Home
Home Rotham	Lt RA	26.87	
Hood	Mr	14.511	father of Capt Alex. Hood and Sir Samuel Hood KB
Hood	Lady	16.88	
Hood	Mr	20.167	Sgn of the Sybille
Hood Alexander	Lord	31.439	Viscount Bridport
Hood W	Lt Col	31.440	
Hood Samuel	V Adm Sir	33.511	at Madras
Hood Samuel	Rt Hon Vis	35.88	at Bath, aged 92 years
Hooker John		23.176	in father's house at Deptford Dockyard
Hooker John		27.440	of the Victualling Office, Cove, Ireland
Hookham Thomas		25.515	
Hooper Thomas		32.163	
Hooper William		32.435	
Hope	Mrs	3.240	wife of R Hope
Hope Henrietta	Miss	5.96	
Hope Charles	Mr	15.87	
Hope Charles	Commissioner	20.256	
Hope Jemima J	Lady	20.256	
Hope W		33.262	

Hope George	R Adm Sir	39.424	
Hope Anne J	Lady	40.243	
Hopkins John	Capt	1.174	
Hopkins R B	Lt RN	26.180	
Hornby	Mrs	27.440	mother of Capt H. RM
Hornsey John		10.175	
Horton Thomas		25.434	
Hoseason G		18.520	
Hotchkis David	Capt	5.280	
Hotchkys Charles	Capt RN	33.88	
Hotham Montagu		13.246	
Hotham William	Adm Lord	29.440	
Houghton Francis		30.87	
Houlton	Mr	25.176	of the Cadmus
Houston	Capt	25.86	of the Vestal
Howard	Lt	14.174	of the Centaur
Howard Robert		26.83	
Howard Thomas		36.258	
Howden Robert		27.352	
Howe	Earl	2.263	
Howe Julian	Hon	9.251	
Howe John		27.511	
Howe	Lord Vis	32.88	
Howe	Capt RM	33.352	at Blackheath
Howell John	Lt	24.515	
Howorth John	R Adm	5.375	
Hubbeck	Mr	25.88	Sgn of the Apelles
Hubbert Michael		33.172	
Huddart John	Capt	13.164	
Huddart Joseph		36.174	FRS
Hudsbal Uriah		13.410	
Hudson	R Adm	9.251	
Hudson	Capt	11.87	of the Chalmers, West Indiaman
Hudson Thomas	Capt HEIC	21.520	
Hudson Thomas		27.511	seaman on Northumberland
Hue	Mrs	24.176	wife of Capt Hue RN
Hue	Capt RN	27.439	of Tamworth
Hughes	Lady	4.348	wife of Adm Sir Edward Hughes KB dec'd
Hughes Edward		13.335	
Hughes	Lady	21.520	widow of Adm Sir Edward H.
Hughes Richard	Capt RN	23.352	son of Adm Sir Richard H.
Hughes Walter		26.433	
Hughes Richard	Adm Sir	27.88	
Hughes Hugh		29.78	
Hughes William		29.512	
Hughes	Mrs	31.352	widow of the late Adm Robert Hughes
Hughes John		40.74	
Hull William		13.410	
Hulsenbos P	Lt	17.341	
Humble Thomas		22.250/1 22.352	
Humphreys	Mrs	20.336	wife of Capt Humphreys

Humphries H	Lt	2.548	
		2.644	
Humphries John		15.257	
Humphries Thomas	Lt RN	27.87	
Hunloke Thomas W		27.88	
Hunt	Mr	1.262	son of William Hunt of Chatham Dock yard
Hunt Anthony	Capt	1.347	
Hunt	Mrs	12.87	widow of Edward Hunt
Hunt	Capt RN	28.513	of the Britomart
Hunt N	Capt	39.423	
Hunter F		2.83	of the Navy Pay Office
Hunter William	Lt	23.176	
Hunter J		27.175	
Hurst Isaac		19.259	
Husband T L		33.512	
Hussey Pane	Lt	5.439	
Hutchins Harriet	Miss	37.86	
Hutchinson Alexander C		21.352	infant son of
Hutchinson Thomas		29.78	
Hutton	Capt	6.172	of the Vesuvius
Hyams Joseph		13.410	
Ibbetson J		12.255	
Ibbetson	Mr	36.440	Mid of the Cornwallis
Impey Elijah	Sir	22.352	
Ingle William	Mr	24.88	
Inglis John	V Adm	17.264	
Inglis	Mrs	30.88	wife of Capt C Inglis
Ingram William	Lt RN	32.170	
Inman	Commissioner	23.176	
		24.439	
Innes David		18.437	
Innes John	Mr	39.88	
Innis Lawrence		9.241	
Insliff George		29.78	
Irby Metheuin E	Hon	22.176	
Ireland John		19.87	
Ireland James		24.439	
Ireland Robert J		27.352	
		27.440	
Ireland	Lt	30.360	of the Thistle
Irwin John	Lt	6.348	
Irwin George	Capt RN	23.440	
Irwin George	Mr	23.440	
Irwin John	Capt RN	27.352	
Isby William		25.164	
Isham John Edmund	Lt RN	23.88	
Ives Henry A	Mr	39.498	
Ivey William		40.74	
Ivie D	Lt RN	36.440	
Jackman	Major Gen	9.498	
Jackson Joseph	Capt RN	3.156	
Jackson W	Capt	9.423	
Jackson G	Mr	16.264	

Jackson Peter		20.250	
Jackson J	Mr	21.352	
Jackson William	Lt RN	24.87	
Jackson Mathew		29.78	
Jackson Charlotte M	Mrs	29.352	
Jackson William		31.83	
Jackson C		33.257	
Jackson John C B	Lt	35.440	
Jacob John		34.512	
Jago	Lt RN	20.336	
James D		18.438	
James John		26.433	
James Tobias		37.168	
Jamieson Thomas		25.175	
Jansenbus Rudolph		31.257	
Jardine	Capt RM	28.88	at Stonehouse
Jardine	Mr	36.258	Mid on the Albion
Jarmain	Mrs	23.88	widow of Lt Jarmain RM
Jarvis George		25.434	
Jarvoise H	Miss	37.264	
Jayms James		30.85	
Jeans	Lt RN	36.174	at Fratton
Jeffery John		26.87	
Jeffries A		3.240	
Jeffrey Samuel		25.433	
Jeffreys John		25.515	
Jeffreys	Mr	36.264	Sgn RN at Whitchurch
Jenkins G	Lt RN	23.170/176	
Jenkins Henry	Capt RN	30.448	
Jenkins H	AB	33.262	on the Endymion
Jenkinson	Capt	18.240	of 95th Regmt
Jenner Robert		24.516	
Jennings Benjamin	Mr	1.176	
Jennings U	Capt	15.264	
Jennings James		16.176	
Jennis Thomas	Lt RN	14.174	
Jervis	Mrs	10.175	aunt of Earl St Vincent
Jervis	Capt RN	13.165	of the Tonnant, nephew of Earl St Vincent
Jervis William		29.264	
Jewell Walter	Lt RN	21.176	
Jocelyn	Capt RN	16.88	
Jocelyn James Bligh	Lt Hon	28.88	
John Abel		32.163	
Johns J		35.86	
Johnson Edmund	Lt RN	5.356	
Johnson W V		16.175	
Johnson	Capt	18.240	of 36th Regmt
Johnson	Capt	18.240	of 87th Regmt
Johnson Henry		21.348	
Johnson Robert		22.251	
Johnson John		25.34	
Johnson	Lt	28.440	of the Bucephalus
Johnson Alexander		29.78	
Johnson John		29.78	
Johnson Robert		32.435	

Johnson Urry	Capt RN	35.264	
Johnston James	Doctor	7.180	
Johnston James	Lt RM	11.87	
Johnston Wm		31.257	
Johnston John F	Lt RN	36.352	
Johnstone Robert	Capt	11.494	
Johnstone	Capt	20.293	of the Perseverance
Johnstone John	Lt RN	21.176	
Johnstone P		23.170	
Johnstone Andrew	Mr	25.176	
Johnstone J N	Capt RN	34.352	
Johnstone J M	Capt RM	34.512	
Jones Henry	Mr	1.348	
Jones Alban	Lt	1.446	
Jones Joseph	Mr	10.87	Purser of the Elephant
		11.494	
Jones C B	Capt RN	13.86	
Jones William		14.167	Marine drummer on Blanche
Jones Samuel		22.259	
Jones Thomas		22.504	
Jones Evan		22.505	
Jones Joseph	Mr	23.520	
Jones George		25.434	
Jones William		26.80	
Jones	Mr	26.264	of the Pitt
Jones Edward		27.506	
Jones Louis		29.258	
Jones Charles		29.348	
Jones John		30.78	Royal Marine on the Berwick
Jones Thomas		30.85	Ord'y Seaman, of the Shannon
Jones Edward		30.176	
		30.264	
Jones Thomas	Capt HEIC	30.360	
Jones N		31.77	
Jones Thomas W	Lt RN	31.262	
Jones Robert		32.435	
Jonhson William		19.259	
Jordan Matthew		20.418	
Joyeuse Villaret	Adm	28.264	of the French Navy
Joze Joaquin		29.78	
Joze de Compass		29.78	
Judd Isaac		28.440	
Jummers William		15.434	
Kain	Sgt RM	32.163	
Kane Christopher		27.351	
Kayton Thomas		29.78	
Kearney Patrick		25.164	
Keast	Mr	33.176	at Plymouth
Keats Richard	Reverend	28.88	
Keele Edward		29.348	
Keeler R	R Adm	24.439	
Keighan Thomas		27.506	
Keile James		35.352	aged 84 years
Kelly William H	V Adm	25.440	
Kelly James		29.78	

Kemp John		24.165	
Kempe	Mrs	35.352	wife of Adm Kempe
Kempenfelt Gustavus A		19.264	
Kempster R S		25.87	
Kempt Francis	Capt	33.512	
Kempthorpe J		4.256	Purser of a ship in ordinary and Lt of the Cornish Miners
Kempthorne	Adm	19.515	
Kenah	Capt RN	33.264	of the Aetna
Kendall	Capt RN	15.264	
Kendrick Edward		24.500	
Kenesick Patrick		15.258	
Kennedy P		8.347	
Kennedy John		15.257	
Kennedy Walter	Mr	25.264	
Kennedy John		30.170	
Kennett	Capt RE	17.86	
Kennicot Charles		29.257	
Kenry Thomas		15.257	
Kent	Mr	5.188	former Tide Surveyor, Portsmouth
Kent Henry	Lt	6.260	
Kent Sarah	Mrs	10.517	see entry for Mrs S Carlisle
Kent	Capt RM	17.432	
Kent R	Capt RM	17.439	
		18.84	
Kent Jane	Mrs	23.176	one of the few women to have travelled twice round the world
Kent William		25.164	seaman of the Boadicea
Kent Thomas W		28.264	RN
Kent Henry	Lt	28.352	at Aboukir Bay in 1801
Kent W	Capt	28.352	of the Unicorn
Kent John	Lt RN	35.176	
Kenyon Thomas		24.504	
Kerbey John	Capt	31.352	
Kerr Jessy	Miss	19.176	
Kerr	Mrs	35.87	at South Sea Common
Khan Mahomed J		24.74	
Kid William H		26.439	of HEIC
Kidd Samuel	Mr	23.520	
Kilbeck	Mr	13.246	of the Diana
Kilner	Capt RN	36.518	at Cockermouth
Kimber William		27.506	
Kindall Bernard	Lt RN	20.419	
King Elizabeth	Mrs	11.87	
King Richard		13.410	
King Richard	Adm Sir	16.514	
King	Capt Hon	19.88	of the Alexandria
King Philip G	Capt RN	20.256	
King W		25.434	
King Henry	Capt	26.179	
King John		29.78	
King	Miss	35.176	niece to Rear Adm Sir George Burlton
King William	Mr	39.343	

Kingsmill Robert	Adm Sir	14.511	
Kingsmill	Miss	20.423	at the seat of her brother, Sir Robert Kingsmill
Kingston John	Lt RM	14.437	
Kinmeer	Lt	2.548	
Kinneer Francis W	Lt RN	6.435	
		6.516	
Kinneer	Adm	25.352	
Kinnier	Lt RN		see F W Kinneer above
Kirby	Mr	33.352	at Cork
Kirby Walter	Lt RN	35.264	
Kirk	Mr	13.166	Sgn RN
Kirk	Mr	25.264	Mid of the Nyaden
Kittoe	Mrs	19.515	wife of Capt Edward Kittoe
Knatchbull Norton J		5.280	RN
Knight J	Mr	16.264	
Knight Thomas		24.331	
Knight W	Capt RN	27.88	
Knight	Capt RN	36.440	
Knight James		36.440	
Knight William	Capt RN	36.518	
Knight	Lt	37.434	of the 11th Regmt
Knighton	Capt RM	4.256	
Knowler G		8.440	
Knowles John	R Adm	5.280	
Knowles James		23.74	
Knowles	Mrs	25.440	wife of John Knowles
		26.87	
Knowles William		32.170	
Knox Edmund		20.253	
Knox Henry		36.174	
Kynaston Charles H		15.258	
Lackey John	Lt RN	12.342	
Lacroix	Monsieur	5.360	of the French Navy
Ladd Abraham		28.82	
Laforey	Miss	15.87	second daughter of Admiral Sir John Laforey
Laird W B		24.264	
Laird	R Adm	28.263	
Lait Anthony		27.506	
Lake John		24.424	
Lake W H	Reverend	27.175	
Lamb Edward	Capt	39.343	
Lambe J	Capt HEIC	9.251	
Lambe John	Lt RN	27.86	
Lambert Arthur		2.247	
Lambert		10.87	infant son of Robert Lambert
Lambert F R		29.263	
Lambert Henry	Capt RN	29.348	
Lambert Charlotte	Mrs	40.243	
Lamond Daniel		5.356	
Lamport	Mr	32.440	Purser RN
Lander George	Lt RM	38.176	
Landers	Vet Sgn	18.240	
Lane Richard	Capt	1.446	

Lane Thomas	Lt RN	14.262	
Lane C H		18.438	
Lane Michael		23.165	
Lane	Lt RN	37.440	at Waterford
Lang	Mr	6.348	gunner of the Saint Antoine
Lang Richard		29.258	
Langara	Adm	15.264	
Langford	Mrs	15.440	wife of Capt Langford RM
Langford James		29.348	
Langford Frederick	Capt RN	33.352	
Langford Wm W		37.440	
Langharne M	Capt RN	23.520	
		24.176	
Langharne	Miss	29.175	daughter of Capt Thomas L.
Langston Joseph	Lt RN	11.263	
Lanyon	Capt RN	39.423	
Laran James W	Lt RN	6.260	
Larcom Thomas	Capt	11.494	
Larcom Joseph	Capt	39.264	
Lark	Mrs	26.352	wife of Henry Lark
Larkan Ann	Mrs	9.498	
Larke	Mrs	18.437	wife of Lt William L.
Larkin George		25.434	
Larmour John	Capt	17.176	
Larwood Joshua	Reverend	19.263	
Laschen Christian	Lt	5.188	
Lash Wm	Mr	39.176	
Lauder Wm		26.515	of the HEIC
Laugharne Martha	Miss	6.84	
Laugharne	Mrs	35.264	mother of Capt W L., R N
Laughlin Michael		29.258	
Laughton James		29.258	
Laurence John	Capt RN	27.264	infant son of
Laurence W R	Major	39.264	
Laurie R	General Sir	12.255	Col, 8th Regmt of Dragoons
Lave	Mrs	38.511	wife of A D Lave
Lavington	Lord	18.347	
Law C	Mr	24.438	
Lawless John		29.258	
Lawrence John		28.359	of the US Frigate Chesapeake
Lawson John		19.342	
Lay John		15.434	
Laydon	Mr	25.88	caulker at Sheerness
Leake W J M	Lt	11.494	
Leake John M		27.88	
Lean Francis		8.176	
Lecale	V Adm Lord	23.264	
		24.263	
Le Cam F	Mr	29.175	
Lechmere William	V Adm	35.86	
Le Cras	Mrs	6.516	widow of Edward Le C.
Leddy	Mr	3.331	Sgn's mate of the Cormorant
Lee John	Capt RN	4.444	
Lee Joseph		21.438	
Lee	Mrs	22.352	wife of Major Richard Lee RM
Lee Margaretta Hay	Mrs	23.519	

Lee M H	Mrs	24.88	
Lee William		37.176	Purser of the Scamander
Lee Wm	Lt	37.264	of signal station Newington
Leeke	Lt	24.440	
Leeson	Mr	39.264	son of the Hon Mrs Leeson
Lefebure William		6.516	
Lefroy Christopher H B		14.165	
Legard Isaac		15.257	
Legeyt Pleydell Dawnay		12.342	
Le Gros	Capt RN	17.440	
Leigh John		22.504	
Le Marchant Thomas		9.166	
Lennox Henry	Lord	27.352	
Lever John		23.352	
Le Vesconte P		17.520	
Leviston Benjamin		16.349	
Lewin Richard		23.176	of HEIC, aged 90 years
Lewington William		14.260	
Lewis James E	Lt RN	6.172	
Lewis William		13.410	
Lewis	Mr	19.515	Asst Sgn of the Warspite
Lewis Richard	Lt RM	22.176	
Lewis George		25.440	
Lewis Christopher		28.82	
Lewis Theophilus	Lt RN	30.88	
Lewis	Mrs	31.352	wife of Commissioner Lewis, Antigua
Liardet	Mrs	13.86	wife of Capt Liardet RM
Lidgbird Henry	R Adm	40.500	
Lilly	Mr	28.440	at Gosport
Lime George		21.343	
Lind	Mrs	34.352	wife of Dr Lind, Sgn of the Warrior
Lind John		37.176	
Lindsay C	Sir	2.82	
		2.172	
Lindsay	Lady	2.548	widow of V Adm Sir John L.
Lindsay	Mrs	34.88	wife of Major Lindsay
Lindsey David		6.147	
Linzee		4.168	wife of Sir H Linzee
Linzee Robert	Adm	12.342	
Lion T	Mr	11.494	
Litchfield	Lt	12.255	of the Renard
Little	Capt RN	5.544	
Littlejohn George		20.419	
Liversage Robert		26.83	
Livesay	Mrs	24.515	wife of John Livesay
Livesey Thomas	Lt	11.494	
Liardet Fred.	Brevet Maj RM	27.87	
Lilburn	Captain	27.515	of the Goshawk
Llewelin John	Reverend	25.352	
Lloyd A Thomas	Lt	1.263	
Lloyd Francis	Lt	4.528	
Lloyd Robert	Lt RN	14.437	
Lloyd J L	Lt	16.88	
Lloyd Merrick		16.175	

Lloyd	Lt	17.264	of the Nile, cutter
Lloyd John		21.260	
Lloyd T H	Lt RN	24.176	
Lloyd Robert		27.351	
Lloyd Hugh		27.506	
Lobb Frederick		16.88	
Lobb William Granville		32.264	
Lock Anthony		25.346	
Lock Nagle	Capt	40.332	
Locke Charles	Capt	3.156	
Locke James	Lt RN	20.256	
Locker William		4.528	Lt Governor, Greenwich Hosp
Lockhart	Adm	3.420	
Lockhart William	Lt	28.513	of 16th Light Dragoon s
Lockwood Peter		26.433	
Lodington	Mrs	20.168	widow of Rev J Lodington
Lodriques Benito		15.258	
Logan W		31.257	
Long Henry	Lt RM	5.356	
Long	Mr	8.88	Purser of the Trent
Long James		30.85	
Long Daniel		36.352	
Longmore William		19.342	
Lops N		23.170	
Lord J	Sgt RM	27.87	
Loring John	Capt RN	20.424	
Losack	Mrs	34.176	wife of Captain Woodley Losack., RN
Lotherington	Mrs	14.262	wife of Capt Lotherington
Louis	Miss	2.448	sister to Capt L. RN
Louis Thomas	R Adm Sir	18.84	
Louis John		34.512	
Love Robert	Lt RN	5.280	
Love Thomas	Mr	14.512	
Love Sarah	Mrs	25.86	
Lovell	Lt	24.263	of the Puissant
Lovell	Lt RN	35.264	
Lovett William		7.276	
Low	Lt	12.432	of the Imogene
Lowcay J W	Lt RM	26.515	
Lowdon	Mr	36.259	Mid of the Leander
Lower Edward		7.532	
Lowry John		22.162	
Lucas	Lt	22.176	of the Dedaigneuse
Lucas	Mr	29.264	Purser of the Ruby
Lucas James		40.73	
Luckey J		9.81	
Lufkin	Lt	5.544	
Luke Oliver		17.343	
Luke	Mrs	30.522	wife of R Adm Luke
Lumsdaine	V Adm	27.176	
Lunce Nimrod		14.167	
Luskin	Lt	6.172	of the Virginia
Lutterell	Mr	18.520	of the Boreas
Lutwidge Skeffinton	Adm	32.264	

Lyall	Capt RN	31.438	at Haslar
		31.512	
Lydiard	Capt RN	19.87	
Lynn Francis	Capt RN	23.440	
Lynn	Lt RM	37.434	
Lyons	Mrs	10.517	sister to Mrs Adm Holloway
Lyons	Mr	12.511	
Lyons John		19.259	
Lyons James		26.433	
Lyons Michael		27.506	
M'Andrew Thomas		16.349	
M'Arthur M'Arthur		22.440	
M'Arthur	Lt RN	33.88	at Haslar
MacBallam	Mr	23.440	Sgn, aged 91 years. Was at Carthagena in 1741 with Tobias Smollet
M'Bride	Adm	3.156	
M'Cann Robert		17.347	
M'Cardel Alexander		23.165	
M'Carthy Felix		20.494	son of
M'Carthy John		26.433	
McClellan John Law		32.264	
M'Clelland T		7.180	
M'Cleverty	Mrs	28.88	wife of H M'Cleverty
M'Clew Matthew		29.348	
M'Clure Robert Kingsmill		25.87	
M'Cormack Neil		16.81	
M'Coy	Mrs	30.448	at South Sea Common
M'Creary D S		19.88	
M'Cromick William		17.343	
M'Cuen Patrick		31.425	
M'Cumming	Mrs	12.166	wife of Capt B M'Cumming
M'Dermist B	Capt	5.280	
M'Donald John	Lt Col RM	1.262	
MacDonald A	Lt RM	12.342	
M'Donald	Lt RN	13.166	of the Lapwing
MacDonald Alex.	Col RM	14.174	
M'Donald James		22.505	
M'Donald Thomas		25.434	
M'Donald James		27.440	
M'Donough James		24.504	
M'Doughall	V Adm RN	32.511	
MacDowall James		33.88	
M'Dowall Robert	Adm	35.264	
M'Evoy John		31.83	
Macey Walter		29.352	
MacFarlane	Mr	25.264	of the Nyaden
MacFarlane James	Lt RN	32.439	
		33.88	
M'Gee James		22.251	
M'George J	Capt RN	39.423	
M'Gourvey James		24.500	
M'Gregor	Ensign	18.240	of the 88th Regiment
M'Gregor Charles		30.81	
M'Innes	Mr	21.520	Asst Sgn of the Ocean

MacIntosh	Capt	27.439	at Wampoo
M'Intyre J	Lt RM	30.88	
M'Ireson John		16.349	
M'Kenza Samuel		29.257	
MacKenzie Colin	Lt	5.187	
MacKenzie Simon	Capt	11.494	
M'Kenzie Kenneth		15.257	
MacKenzie Donald Grant		29.175	
M'Kenzie John		32.163	
MacKey James		2.644	
MacKey William		25.433	
MacKey Alexander	Capt RN	27.88	
MacKie John		22.505	
M'Killop Richard		28.513	
M'Kinlay George		5.356	
M'Mackin Samuel		15.342	
MacKintosh David		14.260	
MacKintosh Alexander		16.79	
MacKrell John	Lt RN	34.88	
M'Laughlin	Mrs	40.243	wife of Bryan M'Laughlin, Surgeon, Greenwich Hosp
M'Laurin	Mrs	8.88	widow of Capt M'Laurin
M'Lean	Mr	6.172	Sgn of the Latona
M'Lean	Lt RN	12.342	
M'Lean D	Lt	22.147	of 3rd Battn, 1st Foot
M'Lean Hector	Lt RN	35.264	
M'Lean R		36.87	
M'Lean	Mr	37.264	pensioned gunner RN
M'Leay James Barclay		24.87	
M'Leary William		7.452	
MacLeod Roderick	Lt	23.440	
M'Leod W H		36.87	
M'Leod	Mrs	40.332	wife of Lt Alexander M'Leod
M'Millan Iver		18.174	
M'Millan	Mr	22.176	Sgn of the Aboukir
M'Millan George	Lt RN	36.352	
M'Millan W	Capt RM	37.264	
M'Mullen James		26.433	
M'Namara James	R Adm	7.276	
M'Neal Donald		28.82	
M'Neil Archibald	Lt	19.264	
M'Queen Wm		28.243	
MacTaggart	Capt RN	2.82	
M'Tavish Donald		34.512	
M'Veigh Patrick	Lt RN	34.176	
M'Vicar Alex. Reid		27.88	
M'Wiggan John		29.78	
Maddock William		26.351	
Maddox Thomas		21.347	
Madgshon John		39.424	
Magin	Doctor RM	27.175	
Mail John		20.418	
Main Robert		5.253	
Maitland Robert		6.260	
Malbon	Mrs	10.350	wife of Capt M. of the Aurora
Malbon Micajah	Capt RN	29.512	

Malbon Samuel	Capt RN	35.264	
Malcom	Mr	6.435	
Malin T		23.175	
Man Robert	Adm	30.264	
Manaton	Mrs	18.85	grandmother of Captains J & H Ommanney
Manderson James	Master	34.440	
Manderston	Lt RN	35.86	of the Shannon
Mandeson John	Lt	1.263	
Manley John L	Capt	38.176	
Mann	Mrs	20.424	wife of Adm Robert Mann
Mann Lawrence		27.506	
Manners W	Capt	32.176	
Manning Robert		3.156	RN
Mansell	Mr	24.516	eldest son of Bishop of Bristol
Mansfield John M	Capt RN	29.440	
Manvers Charles	Earl of	36.87	
March William		22.505	
Mardon Robert		2.548	
Markham William	Rev Doctor	18.437	
Markham	Mrs	24.516	and her infant son. Wife of V Adm Markham
Marnall	Mr	24.440	of Plymouth
Marr	Mr	17.264	Bosun, Plymouth Dock Yard
Marriott James	Sir	9.251	
Mars William		30.240	
Marsden	Mrs	12.255	widow of John M., mother of the Secy to the Admiralty
Marsh George		4.444	
Marsh	Mrs	12.511	widow of Capt Marsh
Marsh William		14.167	
Marsh Edward		14.167	
Marsh Edward	Capt RN	29.175	
Marshall Charles	Lt RN	11.87	55 yrs a Lieutenant in Navy
Marshall	Lt	11.494	
Marshall W		17.264	
Marshall E	Lt	17.520	
Marshall David		24.165	
Marshall	Mr	25.176	of the Amethyst
Marshall Edward		27.176	quarterman, Plymouth
Marshall Edward		27.438	of the HEIC
Marshall	Mr	28.263	former Asst Sgn, Portsmouth Dock Yard
Marshall William		29.258	
Marshall	Mrs	29.512	widow of Elias Marshall
Marsham H S	Lt RN	33.352	
Marshland John		22.256	
Marslin William		16.439	
Marsovick John		21.347	
Marston John	Lt	30.264	
Martin	Monsieur	5.360	of the French Navy
Martin	Mrs	16.352	wife of R Adm Martin
Martin	Lady	19.264	widow of Sir Henry Martin
Martin A		20.253	
Martin	Mr	24.87	at Portsea
Martin George	Capt RM	25.88	

Martin	Mrs	28.263	mother of John Martin of Portsmouth Dockyard
Martin John		37.339	
Martyr Joseph		30.360	
Maskelyne Nevil	Reverend	25.176	Astronomer Royal
Mason	V Adm	7.532	
Mason Lennard		15.258	
Mason James		17.347	
Master Ferry	Mr	32.512	
Matcham Francis		19.263	
Mathews William		25.434	
Mathison H	Mr	16.264	
Matson	Mrs	12.432	wife of Mr C Matson
Matson R		13.166	
Matterface	Lt	32.440	of the Rota
Matthews	Lt	19.176	of the Hunter
Matthews George		22.137	
Matthews William		29.258	
Matthews William	Mr	34.352	RN
Matthews	Capt RM	38.88	at Poole
Matthias Thomas J		29.348	
Maude	Mr	19.176	of the Chichester
Maude George		29.175	
Maude Thomas		29.176	
Maude William		30.360	
Maude Anne	Mrs	40.164	
Maughan James		2.439	
Maughan	Capt	6.348	
Maurice Ferdinand M	Capt	29.88	
Maurice	Mrs	33.512	wife of Capt Maurice RN
Mawdesley Othuel	Lt RN	29.175	
Maxwell Peter		2.644	
Maxwell	Capt	3.240	
Maxwell	Mr	9.423	Mid on the Bellerophen
Maxwell	Mr	13.166	son-in-law of Capt S P Mouat
Maxwell James		25.88	
Maxwell	Mr	28.263	Navy Agent, Barbadoes
May R H		18.438	
May Thomas		29.84	
May Henry		29.440	
May Victor	Lt	32.161	of De Wattesville's Regiment
Maybee Harry	Mr	21.352	
Mayfield John		7.78	
Mead Joseph	Capt RN	2.644	
Meadows Ed		31.257	
Meadows J W		33.440	
Mears William		3.240	of the HEIC
Mechain	the Astronomer	13.86	
Meddal James		29.257	
Medlyn John		21.343	
Medway John Allan	Lt RN	27.88	
Meik James Lind	Lt	9.497	
Meik Lind	Lt RN	39.264	
Mein James	Capt RN	21.176	
Melhuish John	Commander	11.494	
Melkin Elijah		22.137	

Mellegan	Mr	33.512	Sgn of the Tigre
Melsteat	Major	25.346	Danish national
Melville	Lord	25.514	
Mends Charles Bowen		25.515	
Mends	Capt RN	30.264	infant son of
Mends	Mr	36.258	Asst Surveyor on the Albion
Meredith John		29.440	
Meredith Amelia	Miss	39.424	
Merrett John		26.515	
Merritt William		25.440	
Merritt John		27.88	
Metcalf B		3.240	
Metcalfe George		40.74	
Metz Philip		24.255	
Meyler Matthew		16.79	
Michie George		24.88	
Middlemist Thomas		28.263	
Middleton	Mr	24.263	of the Dreadnought
Middleton	Mrs	24.439	widow of Capt M. RN
Middleton Charles	Baron Barham	29.511	
Milbanke Mark	Adm	13.504	
Milbanke	Mrs	28.513	widow of Adm Mark M.
Mildredge M	Lt	24.515	
Mildron John		17.347	
Miles Sam		2.244	
Miles John		21.438	
Millar John	Capt	12.166	of the Russian Navy
Millard Samuel		30.85	
Miller Elizabeth	Mrs	1.176	wife of Capt Simon Miller RN
		1.348	
Miller	Capt	2.448	of the Theseus
Miller John		4.528	
Miller W		7.92	
Miller G		9.81	Surgeon
Miller	Lt RN	9.81	of the Chichester
Miller Frederick		13.410	
Miller Ralph W	Capt RN	19.515	
Miller Robert		20.251	
Miller	Mrs	27.440	wife of Col Miller RM
Miller George	Capt RN	28.439	
Miller William		29.78	
Miller	Mrs	36.87	widow of Lt J F M.RN
Miller William		39.264	
Millichamp John		15.258	
Millman J		32.264	
		32.352	
Millman	Mr	34.440	of the St Domingo
Mills Peter		20.418	
Mills John		28.162	
Mills William		31.503	
Mills John		33.340	
Milne George	Lt	4.421	
Milne	Mrs	32.439	wife of R Adm Milne RN
Milne Alexander		34.352	
Milne James	Capt RN	38.257	
Milne David		40.164	

Milrea William		26.351	
Minchin Paul	R Adm	24.264	
Minchin	Ensign	37.434	
Mingay J		33.172	
Minnifie John		27.439	aged 92 years
Minns Thomas		26.258	
Minster	Lt RM	5.188	
Mitchell	Mrs	4.444	mother of Adm Sir Andrew M.
Mitchell Walter		4.528	of the HEIC
Mitchell John	Mr	13.86	
Mitchell	Capt	14.86	of the Inspector
Mitchell Andrew	V Adm Sir	15.352	
Mitchell W	Lt	17.86	of the 71st Regmt
Mitchell John	Lt RN	27.88	
Mitchell R		33.262	
Mitchell William	V Adm Sir	35.264	
Mitchell William		37.176	Purser, formerly of Gladiator
Mitchell William		40.74	Master on the Queen
Mitford H	Capt	11.494	
Moises Hugh	Reverend	16.88	
Molloy Phillip		29.78	
Molloy Thomas		30.85	
Molloy Anthony J P	Capt RN	32.264	Retired
Molloy Anthony P	Capt RN	34.440	
Moncrieff W W		30.264	
Moncue John	Capt RN	31.352	
Monkton	Mrs	16.88	wife of Capt M. RN
Monkton	Mrs	25.513	wife of Capt M. RN
Monneber Ann Sophia		39.423	
Monro	Mrs	25.440	widow of Lt Col Monro RM
Montagu	Mrs	7.364	wid of the late Adm Montagu
Montagu S	Miss	13.504	
Montagu Ann	Miss	17.176	
Montagu Charlotte	Miss	27.86	
Montagu James	Capt RN	40.74	
Monteith	Major RM	23.520	
Montgomerie Roger	Lt the Hon	1.446	
Montgomery Walter	Sgn RN	2.548	
Moodie James	Lt RN	31.172	
Moody Edmond James		18.174	
Moody Thomas		18.348	
Moody Geo. Wentworth		24.516	
Mooney Edward		16.81	
Moore J	Capt RN	9.498	
Moore William		15.258	
Moore John		15.434	
Moore George	Mr	21.520	
Moore	Mrs	22.88	mother of A Moore, master-smith, Plymouth Dock Yard
Moore Richard	Mr	24.176	at Portsea, aged 90 yrs
Moore Henry		30.250	
Moore T W		33.340	
Moorsom	Capt	29.84	of the Princess Amelia
Moorsom	Mrs	35.176	widow of Richard M.
Moreton John		22.137	
Moreton Anne Louisa	the Hon	25.352	

Morgan Henry	Mid	14.429	of the Mars	
		14.437		
Morgan William		15.257		
Morgan John		25.432		
Morgan	Mr	26.433	of Portsea	
Morgan Thomas		28.166		
Morgan William M	Lt RM	36.259		
Morgan	Mrs	40.500	wife of Rev T M., Chaplain to Portsmouth Dock Yard	
Moriaty Edward		28.162		
Moriaty John		30.85		
Morice Richard	Capt RN	23.520		
Morin Tirel		6.260		
Morres Lodge F	Lt	20.424	of 22nd Regmt of the Foot	
		20.495		
Morris Edward		2.439		
Morris	Mrs	6.260	widow of Capt M. and mother of Capt Nichol Morris RN	
Morris Amherst	Capt RN	7.452		
Morris	Capt	24.176	at Plymouth	
Morris Henry		31.175		
Morris George	Capt RN	32.440		
Morris	Capt RN	33.87	at Cambleton	
Morrison John		10.509		
Morrison	Lt RM	14.428	of the Hero	
Morrison James		15.257		
Morrison Thomas		27.506		
Morrison John		31.176	and his wife Elizabeth Wallace 53 yrs married	
Morrisay William		30.85		
Mortlock Lewis	Capt	1.176		
Mosberry	Mrs	15.176	wife of R Mosberry	
Moss Sarah	Mrs	28.440		
Mosse Robert	Capt	5.356		
Mosse	Capt RN	5.376		
Mosse Mary Ann	Miss	31.352		
Motherwell Matthew		30.360		
Mouat S P	Capt	13.166		
Mouat S P	Capt	13.166	his two youngest daughters	
Mould Jacob P		27.506		
Moulden	Miss	9.81	sister to R Adm Cooper	
Mouteney J B		22.137		
Mountney Wm Barclay		22.176		
Mowatt	Lt RN	10.175	of the Ulysses	
Mowbray William		29.264		
Moyase James		18.252		
Mudge J	Mr	11.175		
Mudge	Lt	19.263		
Mugg Francis John		14.437		
Muir John		15.257		
Muir Robert		26.515		
Mulcaster	Lt RN	13.165	son of Major Gen M. RE	
Mullins Thomas		14.167		
Mullins Charles		31.439		
Munn T C	Capt RN	33.352		
Munroe	Col RM	10.350		

Murche	Monsieur	5.361	of the French Navy
Murphy Jeremiah		13.410	
Murphy James		15.434	
Murphy John		17.343	
Murphy	Mr	23.88	of the Helder
Murphy P		23.176	
Murphy Bartholomew		24.168	
Murphy John	Lt RN	26.351	
Murphy James		26.433	
Murphy William		27.507	
Murphy Michael		30.85	
Murphy Dennis		32.170	
Murphy S		33.262	
Murray Wm		10.263	Sgn, Woolwich Dock Yard
Murray	Lt	11.494	
Murray James		23.165	
Murray Thomas		27.88	
Murray John		27.507	
Musgrave John	Mr	25.264	
Nagle	Mr	23.88	of the Europe, prison ship
Nailor	Lt	8.352	of the Sensible
Nairne John	Capt	18.348	
Nankivel Thomas James		29.78	
Nankivel John		29.84	
Napier Patrick	Capt Hon	5.544	
Napier Charles	Hon	18.520	
Napier F	Lt RN, Hon	32.439	
Nares John Bever		24.352	
Narracott	Mrs	34.512	widow of John Narracott
Narricott	Mrs	35.87	widow of J N Narricott
Naseby John		15.257	
Nash William		25.341	
Nash James		25.434	
Nason Arthur Hyde	Lt	18.268	
Nassey Bernard		20.168	
Neales William		28.439	
Neate Suett Martin		30.360	
Neesham	Mrs	20.256	wife of Capt Neesham RN
Neil John		31.257	
Nelham Abraham		40.74	
Nelson Maurice		5.376	
Nelson	V Adm, Lord Viscount	14.437	
Nelson John		21.347	
Nelson Horatio	Mid	27.264	of the Endymion
Nelson	Mr	30.115	master shipwright, Deptford
		30.176	
Nelson	Mr	32.439	at Jersey, late master of the Victory
Nelthorpe Isaac		26.261	
Nepean Thomas	Major Gen	36.518	RE
Nepeeker	Mr	20.168	Surgeon
Netherwood Titus		20.251	
Nevill John		27.515	

Name		Rank	Ref	Notes
Neville	Martin	Capt RN	10.350	of the Port Mahon
			10.440	
Neville	Samuel	Lt	11.494	
Neville	John		15.258	
Neville	John	Lt	40.74	of the Queen's Regmt
Newby	William		24.255	
Newell	Joshua		29.78	
Newell	John	Lt RN	36.264	
Newhouse		Capt RN	10.517	
Newman		Mr	25.176	sailmaker at Portsmouth
Newman	John		25.432	
Newman	James N	Capt RN	27.88	
Newshim	J		12.166	
Newson		Mr	32.440	at Portsmouth
Newstub	Anthony		29.258	
Newton	John	Lt RN	9.166	
Newton	Thomas	Capt RN	28.440	
Nicholas	Thomas	Lt RN	25.87	
Nicholl	J A	Lt	3.516	
Nicholl	I A	Lt	4.168	
Nicholl	Richard		20.168	
Nicholls	David		17.347	
Nicholls	Thomas		20.253	
Nichols	John		14.167	
Nichols	Robert		29.79	
Nicholson	Robert		3.80	
Nicholson	Alexander		5.356	
Nicholson	James		13.165	
Nicholson		Mrs	20.494	wife of George Nicholson
Nicholson	James	Capt RN	22.440	
Nicholson	G W		36.87	
Nicholson	R (Senior)	Lt RN	37.518	
Nightingale	E	Sir	13.164	
Nind	George		14.437	
Nisbett	Anne	Miss	30.88	
Noble	George		12.87	
Noble	Robert		17.515	
Noble	Andrew		24.516	
Norman		Mrs	5.96	wife of Capt Norman RN
Norman		Capt RM	15.176	
Norman	James	Capt RN	16.514	
Norman		Lt RN	25.264	
Norman		Mr	31.348	Sgn of the Martial
Norman		Lt RN	32.440	of the Rota
Norman	John		33.166	
North	Wm		28.439	aged 95 years
Northcote		Lt RM	20.167	of the Melampus
Northcote	Charles		35.175	
Norton	Robert		25.264	
Norton	John	Lt RN	27.88	
Norton	Hugh		29.258	
Norton	M		33.262	
Norway	J A		31.176	
Nosely		Lt RN	12.255	
Noski	L		30.80	
Notley	John	Mr	18.437	Surgeon

Nott Edward		16.81	
Notter	Mrs	9.251	wife of Lt Notter RN
Nourse Charles		27.345	
Nowell William	Lt RN	24.87	
Noyce James	Capt RN	29.352	
Noyes John		34.88	
Oades Lewis		14.437	
Oakenden H F		32.264	
Oakes	Lt	1.263	of the HMS Resistance
Oakes J	Capt	20.168	
Oakes William	Lt RN	24.438	
Oakley R	Capt RN	33.176	
Oakyey Robert		13.335	
Oates Martin		15.258	
O'Beirne B	Doctor	29.88	
Obel	Lt	25.346	Danish national
O'Brien	Mrs	7.180	wife of Capt O'Brien RN
O'Brien John	Capt RN	11.175	
O'Brien Edward	R Adm	21.88	
O'Brien Terence		24.440	
O'Brien	Lady Edward	24.515	
O'Brien	Mr	36.174	of the Antelope
O'Brien	Rt Hon Lady	37.440	
O'Bryen	Mrs	17.352	wife of R Admiral O'Bryen
O'Connelly John		30.85	
Odell	Mr	27.87	Sgn of the Scipion
Ogilvie	Lt RN	19.263	
Ogle Chaloner	Adm Sir	36.264	
O'Keefe	Major	25.256	of the 12th Regiment
Oldfield	Major RM	2.172	
Oliphant John	Lt RN	24.88	
Oliver William		22.137	
Ommaney Cornthwaite	R Adm	5.280	
Ommanney Edward		25.87	
Ommanney	Mrs	29.264	widow of Admiral Ommanney
Ommanney Edm. W	Master	29.440	
Onslow Matthew Richard		20.167	
Onslow Richard	Sir	39.88	
Orde	Capt	15.264	of the Nimrod
O'Reilley Dowell	Capt RN	35.516	
Orfur Abdiel	Lt RN	34.512	
Ormerod	Mr	33.87	of the Scipion
Ormiston William		26.88	
Ormsby George	Capt RN	5.187	
Ormsby C C	Lt RN	24.516	
Orrock	Mrs	4.168	widow of Capt Orrock
Orrock	Mr	24.515	gunner of the Pearlen
Orton John	Capt RM	24.439	
Orton	Lt	27.176	of the Ceres
Osborne George		27.345	
Osborne	Lt	34.512	Naval Hospital Plymouth
Osborne Samuel	Adm	36.264	
Osborne Alexander	Mr	39.343	
O'Shaughnessy Edw.	Capt RN	39.264	
Osmond James	Lt RN	27.515	

Otway	Capt RN	11.263	infant son of
Otway William A	V Adm	34.176	
Otway Henry		34.352	
Otway	Mrs	36.264	widow of Admiral W A Otway
Ourry Richard	R Adm	3.156	Retired
Outon	Mrs	29.440	wife of J G Outon
Overind Edward		30.259	
Overton Edward		14.437	
Owens Roland		25.434	
Packwood	Doctor	5.280	
Padeson E	Lt RN	16.514	
Pafoot J W		40.332	
Page John		9.251	Purser
Page	Mrs	10.175	wife of Mr Page of the Sick & Hurt Office
Page John	Mid	12.431	
Page John		38.511	
Paget W	Reverend	1.176	Sec'y to the late Lord Rodney
Paine John		28.161	
Paine Ralph		28.263	
Painter Peter		4.168	RM
Paisley Thomas	Adm Sir	20.494	
Pakenham John	V Adm	18.520	
Pakenham William	Capt RN, Hon	27.88	
Palgrave Robert		13.86	
Palmer	Capt RN	3.420	
Palmer William	Lt	5.253	
Palmer Alexander		14.437	
Palmer	Mr	25.88	caulker at Sheerness
Palmer Joseph		25.514	
Palmer John		40.164	
Pancass	Mr	23.176	carpenter RN, aged 90
Paole William		28.162	
Pardoe John		26.83	
Parish John		25.164	
Parke T	Lt	13.504	
Parke George		18.348	
Parke	Mrs	40.332	wife of Capt Edw. P., RM
Parker		2.83	father of the late mutineer
Parker E T	Capt RN	6.259	
Parker William	V Adm Sir	9.81	
Parker	Lady	9.81	wife of Sir P Parker
Parker Christopher	V Adm	11.493	
Parker Hyde	Sir	17.263	
Parker Thomas		17.264	at Boston, USA
Parker Frederick	Capt RN	22.176	
		22.352	
Parker John		22.251	
Parker Edmund		24.87	
Parker	Mr	24.263	of Gosport
Parker William		24.433	
Parker	Mr	25.161	of the Africaine
Parker Reginald	Mr	25.263	
Parker Peter	Adm Sir	27.88	
Parker Elizabeth	Mrs	27.88	

Parker	Lt	28.88	of the Mackerel
Parker Peter	Capt RN, Sir	32.352	
		32.435	
Parker George	Master	36.440	
Parkin	Mr	34.352	of the Endymion
Parkin John		34.352	aged 83 years
Parkyns Augustus	Lt RN	25.176	
Parr William	Lt RN	35.440	
Parrey Robert	Capt RN	20.256	
Parry Paul		9.165	
Parry Francis	V Adm	10.517	
Parry David		16.169	
Parry W		30.264	
Parry	Mrs	32.352	widow of Adm Francis Parry
Parry Edward		32.439	
Parson William		36.264	
Parsons George		27.352	
Pascoe William B	Lt RN	16.176	
Pascoe William R	Lt RN	29.257	
		29.264	
Passmore Henry	Capt	24.352	
Pater C J	Lt RM	22.88	
Pater	Mrs	39.87	wife of R Adm Charles D Pater
Pater Charles D	R Adm	39.176	
Paterson Mary Ann	Miss	21.520	
Paterson David	Capt RN	30.360	
Patey	Miss	23.88	dau of Lt Patey RN
Patten	Major RM	24.88	
Patten Wm	Lt RN	34.88	
Patterson John		16.349	
Patterson Thomas		20.418	
Patterson Michael		22.157	
Patterson William		25.433	
Pattison	Capt RN	30.448	of the Fox
Patton	Mrs	33.512	mother of Lt Jas. H Patton RM
Patton Phillip	Adm	35.87	
Paul	Capt	13.335	of the Pheasant
Paul W		33.257	
Paul C	Capt RN	36.518	
Paulet Henry		12.166	
Pavey	Mr	6.435	of the Centurion
Payler Francis R	Mr	1.88	
Payne Philip		7.92	
Payne Richard	Lt RN	8.352	
Payne Willett	R Adm	10.438	
Payne Robert	Lt RN	14.174	
Payne Robert		20.419	
Payne J	Capt	30.264	
Payne William		33.176	infant son of
Peach	Mrs	28.263	widow of Rev S Peach
Peake	Capt RM	21.264	
Pearce John		13.410	
Pearce John		25.87	
Pearce	Lt	26.351	of the Arethusa
Pearce W		30.522	of the Thais
Pearse John		29.440	

Pearse Richard		37.168	
Pearson R	Sir	13.86	
Pearson	Lady	36.87	widow of Sir Richard Pearson
Pecking	Lt RM	25.176	
Peed J	Lt	28.440	
Peers John Consett	Capt	1.261	
Peers	Capt RM	11.494	
Peers James		15.352	
Pellew	Miss	27.87	daughter of Samuel Pellew
Pellew Edward	Lt RN	37.86	
Pellowe	Mrs	27.440	wife of Capt Pellowe RN
Pelly Charles	Capt RN	27.439	
Pemberton	Mr	10.350	Mid on the Leviathan
Pemberton Isaac		26.264	
Pen	Mr	36.174	Harbour master and King's Pilot of Plymouth
Pender	Mrs	38.348	wife of Francis Pender
Pendergrass Peter		23.74	
Pendergrast	Lt RN	32.352	of the Avon
Penfold	Mrs	27.515	wife of L Penfold
Pengelly John	Capt RN	23.520	
Penny John		37.518	
Percival	Miss	21.264	sister of Lt Thomas Percival
Peregrine Hugh		26.433	
Perkins	Lt Gen RM	9.423	
Perkins John	Capt RN	27.351	
Perkins Wm	Lt RM	27.439	
Perkins	Capt RN	28.88	at Jamaica
Perkins T	Capt RN	33.352	
Perks John		1.433	
Perot Piere		25.432	
Perren James		32.435	
Perry E		18.520	
Perryman William		23.165	
Pessey Thomas		21.348	
Peterson John		28.348	
Peterson Peter		33.352	
Petley	Mrs	29.352	wife of Lt Petley RN
Pettet James	Lt RN	30.88	
Peyton Joseph	Adm	12.256	
Peyton	Mrs	12.256	wife of Adm Joseph Peyton
Peyton	Mrs	21.176	wife of R Adm Peyton
Peyton John	R Adm	22.176	
Peyton Joseph	R Adm	35.352	
Phelan	Mr	40.243	Purser of HMS Semiramis
Phenne Thomas		15.257	
Philip Arthur	Adm	32.352	
Philips John		25.164	
Philips John	Capt RN	29.352	
Philips Thomas		31.77	
Phillimore George	Lt	19.86	
Phillips	Mrs	3.80	wife of Major Phillips RM
Phillips Henry		3.331	
Phillips Philip		27.176	
Phillips	Mrs	27.439	widow of William Phillips
Phillips	Mrs	32.440	widow of Capt D Phillips RN

Phillips James	Mr	39.264	Ld Nelson's Boatswain
Phillps Frances	Mrs	25.87	
Phipps Henrietta S	the Hon	20.494	
Phipps David	Capt RN	26.87	
Pickernel Thomas	Lt RN	35.352	
Pickmore	Mrs	6.84	
Pickmore Francis	V Adm	39.343	
Pierce	Lt	12.342	of the Hippomenes
Pierce James		13.410	
Pierce	Capt HEIC	16.352	
Pierce	Mrs	17.440	widow of Capt Pierce HEIC
Pierce Thomas	Lt RM	25.264	
Pierce Mary Anne	Miss	27.440	
Piercy R	Capt RN	33.352	
Pierrepont	R Adm	30.176	
Pierrepont Charles	Master	31.512	
Pierrepont Maria	Miss	32.176	
Pierson	Capt	4.168	
Pierson John		29.78	
Pigot	Mrs	26.88	widow of Adm Hugh Pigott
Pigott	Mrs	22.440	late widow of Admiral Clarke Gayton
Pigott	Mrs	25.440	widow of Adm Pigott
Pilcher	Capt RM	6.516	
Pilkington	Mid	33.340	of the Seahorse
Pillipan William		29.78	
Pinhorn John		36.440	
Pipon Peter		17.336	
Pitt	Mrs	9.165	wife of Lt Pitt RM
Pitt Thomas		38.348	
Pitts William		14.437	
Pitts Frederic		32.264	
Plank Frederick		17.347	
Plum George		28.162	
Plunket Lawrence		17.343	
Pocock Margaret	Mrs	10.175	
Pocock Isaac	Sir	24.352	
Pocoke G H A		36.259	
Pokes William		22.348	
Pole Charles M	Sir	30.87	
		30.176	
Pollard W		28.88	
Pollock	Dr	39.343	Sgn of the Dromedary
Ponsonby J M	Capt RN	34.512	
Pooke James		6.502	
Pool Joseph		21.438	
Poor John		20.336	
Pope Alexander		12.255	
Pope John	Lt RN	29.257	
		29.264	
Popham Edmund		22.520	
Porteous James		38.348	
Porter R E		4.348	
Porter John G		19.259	
Porter John		26.261	
Portlock Nathaniel	Capt RN	38.264	

Potter John		23.170	
Potter Leonard	Capt	27.515	of the 28th Regmt
Poulden	Mrs	24.439	wife of Mr Poulden of Portsmouth Dock-yard
Poulson Henry		6.62	
Powell	Mr	6.435	of the Centurion
Powell Edmund	Lt RN	25.514	
Powell William		32.435	
Powelson Adiel		6.62	alias Henry Poulson
Powlett	Countess	25.263	
Powys Charles	Hon	12.342	son of Lord Lilford
		12.432	
Pratman John		26.440	
Pratt John		2.644	
Pratt Thomas		28.348	
Pratt G	Lt RN	33.340	
Pratt R	Mid	36.259	on the Granicus
Prattley William		33.341	
Prescott	Capt	20.423	aged 95 years
Preston Robert	Capt RN	38.88	
Prevost Ann	Mrs	22.440	
Prevost Fanny-S	Mrs	29.176	
Price John		9.239	
Price	Mrs	12.166	wife of Capt Price of Abundance
Price	Mrs	16.88	widow of Capt John Price HEIC
Price Thomas		16.439	
Price	Lt	19.176	of the Firefly
Price Samuel	Mr	21.176	
Price John		22.251	
Price Josiah	Capt HEIC	23.88	
Price John	Capt RN	28.88	infant son of
Price Charles P	Capt RN	28.440	
		29.88	
Price	Mrs	31.176	wife of John Price RN
Price	Capt RN	40.243	of St Hilier's, Jersey
Prince Charles	Capt	2.448	
Prince James		20.494	
Pringle Thomas	V Adm	9.498	
		10.517	
Pringle	Mr	19.264	of the Diamond
Prior Edward	Lt RM	15.434	
Prior	Capt	31.439	daughter of
Pritchard William	Mr	23.520	
Pritchard Thomas		25.434	
Pritchard Samuel P		30.360	
Proby Charles	Mr	1.446	
		2.83	
Proby	Capt Lord	12.511	
Prothers William		3.315	
Prout George		25.87	
Prowse	Mr	27.351	former master attendant at Woolwich
Prutz	Captain	25.346	Danish national
Pulham T	Capt RN	9.251	
Pulling	Capt RN	11.168	
Purcell John J		32.439	

Purnel John		28.166	
Purvis R	Capt RN	7.452	
Pye	Miss	5.376	
Pyke John		39.264	
Pywell Elmer	Lt RN	8.520	retired
The Queen		40.414	
Sophia Charlotte Caroline			
Quin T	Mr	18.174	Surgeon
Quin H	Asst Sgn	22.150	of the 71st Foot
Quinn William		24.168	
Quinn James		25.434	
Quinton George		20.251	
Radcliffe	Mrs	25.263	wife of Rev George Radcliffe
Radcliffe Charles		33.79	
Rainier Daniel		7.276	
Rainier	Adm	19.352	
Rallack	Lt	25.515	of the Basilisk
Ralph Thomas		13.335	
Ralt Cornelius		30.442	
Ram Thomas		5.356	
Ram William	Lt RN	14.437	
Ram W A	Lt	14.511	
Ram	Lt RN	21.264	drowned at Bermuda
Ramage E	Capt RN	16.88	
Ramsay John		19.88	aged 125 years
Ramsay David	Lt RN	35.86	
Ramsey Benjamin M		27.440	
Randall	Mr	8.264	proprietor of the Dockyard Dept
Ranelagh	Earl of	4.528	
		5.96	
Raner J P	Mr	11.494	
Ranet Michael G		23.520	
Rankin	Mrs	15.176	wife of J Rankin
Ratford Jenkin		28.363	
Rathborne Samuel		25.433	
Ratrey Robert	Lt RN	31.262	
Ratsey	Mrs	29.352	wife of Lt Robert R. RN
Rawlence R	Lt RN	40.74	
Rea	Lt	28.352	of the Braave
		28.440	
Rea	Major RM	35.352	at Chatham
Read John	Lt	1.348	
Read Roddam A		14.512	
Read	Lt RM	19.176	of the Daedalus
Read John	Lt RM	21.342	
Read J		33.262	
Ready Henry	Lt RN	28.348	
Reardon George		30.78	
Reddeh Edward		29.440	
Reddish Edward	Lt RN	4.348	retired
Redford Ebenezer	Mr	25.176	
Redmore Nicholas		30.259	
Redpath William		13.165	
Reed John		16.81	

Reed James	Mr	21.520	
Reeve Clara	Mrs	18.520	
Reeve	Lt RN	37.86	of the Rochfort
Reeves Charles		27.345	
Reeves	Mr	38.88	late gunner of the Victory
Reid David	Lt	1.263	
Reid	Lt	12.341	of the Victory
Reid Jacob		16.79	
Reid Thomas		16.79	
Reid John		18.438	
Reid John	Lt RM	21.352	
Reid S Legg		30.522	
Reid Sheppard		37.88	
Rendeck John F		24.165	
Renfrey W	Lt RM	36.259	
Rennie George	Lt RN	5.376	
Rennie	Lt RN	22.161	of the Marlborough
		22.176	
Renou A	Capt	13.166	
Renton	Capt	1.262	of HM Sloop Martin
Resen Jan H		17.341	
Retalick	Lt RN	11.87	
Rex	Corporal	28.162	
Reynolds	Lt RM	1.348	
Reynolds Barley	Lt	3.156	
Reynolds	Capt RN	12.432	son of Carthew R.
Reynolds Wm		40.164	
Rice William M		4.528	
Rice Charles	Lt RN	7.276	
Rice Henry	Lt RN	20.336	
Rich John		2.439	
Rich Thomas	Sir	9.339	
Rich Anne	Lady	20.256	
Richards Thomas S	Lt	11.494	
Richards	Lt	13.165	Impress Service, at Poole
Richards William		18.71	
Richardson	Capt	15.87	of the Utile
		15.176	
Richardson Mervan		15.258	
Richardson	Mr	25.87/175	of the Hussar
Richardson Harriet	Mrs	26.264	
Richardson James		27.345	
Richardson	Mrs	27.440	wife of Lt W R. RN
Richardson	Mrs	33.352	widow of the late dispenser of Haslar Hospital
Richardson Henry	Capt RN	35.87	
Richardson Wm	Capt RN	40.164	
Richery	R Adm	1.348	
Rickerby Thomas		31.425	
Ricketts William		19.342	
Rickords George	Lt	1.348	
Ridgeway David		15.257	
Ridgway John		21.343	
Ridley James		13.410	
Riley James		7.85	
Riley	Mr	9.423	Sgn of the Diomede

Riley Richard		19.176	
Rios Joseph de Mendoza		35.352	of the Spanish Royal Navy
Riou Edward	Capt	5.356	
Riou	Capt	5.376	
Risk Michael		30.353	
Ritchie A	Capt	24.352	
Rivers James E	Lt RN	33.88	
Robb Jane	Miss	23.176	
Robb Charles	Capt RN	29.264	
Robbin George	Capt RN	31.439	
Roberg Mathias		23.513	
Roberts Hugh		3.502	
Roberts John		23.352	at Trethill, Cornwall
Roberts William	Capt RN	25.176	
Roberts John		26.433	AB on the Galatea
Roberts Charles	Capt RN	34.352	aged 96 years
Robertson Benjamin		4.528	Justice of the Peace
Robertson John		24.176	
Robertson	Mr	24.263	of the Dreadnought
Robertson William		26.87	
Robertson James M	Capt	26.515	
Robertson T		27.439	
Robins J	Mr	24.439	
Robins	Mrs	34.176	wife of Lt FL Robins RN
Robins	Lt RN	36.352	of the Bermuda
Robinson Mark	R Adm	2.548	
Robinson Edward		5.440	
Robinson William		9.251	
Robinson William		15.257	
Robinson Robert		16.349	
Robinson James		16.439	
Robinson John	R Adm	18.347	
Robinson George	Lt	24.515	
Robinson	Mrs	25.86	wife of Adm Mark Robinson
Robinson Rowland		32.435	
Robinson	Mrs	36.87	wife of Capt Robinson RN
Robinson C	Lt RN	36.440	
Robinson Wm	Lt RN	37.352	aged 82 years
Robson W		24.164	
Robson Edward		30.264	
Roby	Mrs	17.440	wife of Capt Fasham RN
Roby Fasham	Capt	19.515	
Roche Thomas O		12.317	
Roddam	Mrs	18.174	wife of Adm Robert Roddam
Roddam Robert	Adm	19.352	
Rodgers Wm		31.257	
Roe Henry		5.188	
Rogers Jonathan	Doctor	26.88	former physician to the Imperial Russian Fleet
Rogers J		26.179	agent for French PoW's
Rogers Robert		28.348	
Rogers	R Adm	32.352	at Tours in France
Rogers William		32.435	
Rolf William		28.82	
Rolland Peter	Capt HEIC	39.424	

Rollo James	Lt RN	9.165	
Rooke N	Lt	11.494	
Rooke William		15.434	
Rooney John		25.433	
Rory David	Lt RM	31.87	
Rose Jos.		5.356	
Rose	Mrs	23.88	wife of Lt James Rose RN see also **23**.176/264
Rose Edward H		24.176 24.264	
Rose Richard	Mr	25.175	
Rose George	Rt Hon	39.87	
Rosenhagen P L	Capt RN	29.440	
Rosewell	Mr	24.175	at Greenwich
Rosilia G		22.251	
Roskruge Francis	Lt	14.437	
Ross John		2.82	
Ross	Miss	2.172	daughter of Sir J Ross of Balnagown
Ross A J	Capt-Lt RM	5.188	
Ross W		6.348	
Ross J	Lt RN	9.165	
Ross W	Lt	14.511	
Ross John		15.258	
Ross Thomas	Lt RN	17.352	
Ross D		20.168	
Ross John	Lt Col	22.176	
Ross John		26.343	seaman on the Naiad
Ross George	Capt RN	29.352	
Ross Charles	Lt Gen Sir	31.176	
Ross	Miss	39.264	infant dau of Capt CBH R. RN
Ross Francis	Lt RN	40.74	
Rowan	Mr	12.511	Surgeon
Rowan David		20.80	
Rowan Frederick H		26.87	
Rowe Thomas		15.257	
Rowe Edward		21.438	
Rowe	Capt RN	40.332	of the Island of Barbadoes
Rowlands Esther	Mrs	37.440	
Rowley	General	18.268	
Rowley Bartholomew S	Adm	22.441 26.439	
Rowley	Dow.Lady	29.88	
Rowley Edward	Capt RN	38.348	
Roxburgh	Mr	6.147	master on the Pompee
Royal George		15.434	
Rudhall	Lt RN	24.515	of the Armada
Rule William	Sir	34.512	
Rushworth Edward	Capt RN	28.264	
Rushworth Edward		38.348	
Russel	Mrs	39.264	wife of R Adm Russel
Russell James	Capt RN	6.516	
Rutherford Alexander		6.157	
Rutherford George		19.515	
Rutherford	Col	30.176	
Rutherford W G	Capt RN	39.88	

Ryan Edward		16.349	
Ryan John		36.440	
Rymer Charles H		25.264	
Ryves	Mrs	32.439	mother of Capt G T Ryves RN
Ryves H E	Reverend	38.176	
Sabday		13.410	
Sader Dominique		30.85	
St George William M	Lt RN	14.437	
St Vincent	Countess of	35.176	
Salmon S W	Mr	21.176	
Salmon Peter	Mr	24.176	
Salmon William		33.340	
Salmond William		29.348	
Salter George E	Lt RN	10.350	
Salter Harry	Lt RM	27.88	
Salter	Lt RN	37.352	at Portsmouth
Sampson I		25.87	
Sampson	Lt RM	39.498	
Samuel Charles		29.348	
Samwell David	Mr	1.175	Surgeon RN
Samwell W	Capt	36.264	
Sanderson R B		38.88	
Sandes J T		32.435	
Sandford Thomas	Mr	6.84	
Sandys Edwin	Lt	5.356	
Sandys George	Lt RN	28.513	
Sandys Charles	R Adm	31.511	
Sandys	Lt RN	36.87	
Sandys Elizabeth	Mrs	36.87	
Sangter Joseph		30.442	
Saradine	Mrs	11.421	wife of Capt Saradine RN
Saradine	Capt RN	13.166	
Sanfernal	Monsieur	5.361	of the French Navy
Sapenack Alexander		15.257	
Saul Patrick		16.439	
Saumarez	Mrs	8.440	sister-in-law of Admiral Sir John Saumarez
Saumarez Mary	Miss	28.439	
Saumarez Carteret	Miss	32.176	
Saunders William		22.505	
Saunders Abraham		27.345	
Saunders Richard	Capt RN	32.439	aged 86 years
Saunders Andrew	Capt RN	33.88	
Saunders Alexander	Capt	40.73	
Saunderson John		27.506	
Saunderson Thomas		36.352	
Saunier	Monsieur	5.360	of the French Navy
Sause Richard		17.264	
Savage	Mrs	23.264	wife of V Adm Savage
Savage	Capt	27.439	of the Borner
Saville	Capt RN	12.341	Agent for Prisoners at Jamaica
Sawyer	Mr	12.342	Captain's clerk of Inflexible
Sawyer	Adm	26.87	his eldest son
Sawyer	Mrs	33.352	widow of the late Adm Sawyer
Saxton Charles	Sir	20.423	

Name	Rank	Ref	Note
Sayer George	Capt RN	27.351	
		27.440	denial of death
Sayer Charles		36.174	
Scafe John		27.176	
Schabner	Lt RN	37.86	at Martinique
Schmidt Carl		29.348	
Schomberg Catharine Anna	Mrs	11.87	
Schomberg Alexander	Sir	11.344	
Schomberg Isaac	Capt RN	29.175	
Scofield John		20.418	
Scotland Thomas C	Lt RN	29.263	
Scott M H	Capt RN	11.494	infant son of
Scott John		14.437	
Scott	Capt	18.520	of the Boreas
Scott	Mrs	18.520	wife of Capt Scott of Boreas
Scott Robert		20.418	
Scott H M	Capt RN	21.88	infant daughter of
Scott Alexander	R Adm	25.440	
Scott William		29.258	
Scott John		32.440	
Scriven Thomas		14.437	
Seaford Jacob		15.257	
Seager Thomas		24.168	
Sealey F A		22.352	
Searle George		29.264	
Seater	Capt RN	16.88	of the Mediator
Sebastian James		25.432	
Seccombe Thomas	Capt RN	19.352	
Seggess James		21.348	
		21.352	
Sego Louis J		27.506	
Segona Nicholas		28.162	
Selby William	Capt RN	25.515	
Selby Thomas		30.85	
Selsey John	Rt Hon Lord	36.87	
Sempell Thomas		24.515	
Senior Christopher	Lt RN	36.264	
Seppings Robert		38.511	
Sergess James			see Seggess, James
Serle Ambrose		28.264	
Serle H H	Lt	30.522	
Sermon David		22.264	aged 106 years. Sailed with Anson on the Centurion
Serra Peter A	Mr	18.437	
Seward	Lt	12.166	of the Renard
Seward	Mrs	29.264	wife of Capt Seward RN
Sewell Henry		5.188	
Sewell	Mr	8.440	bookseller of Cornhill
Seymour Horatia	Lady	6.84	
Seymour Hugh	V Adm Lord	6.435	
Seymour P	Capt	10.517	aged 84 years −74 of which he served in the Navy
Seymour Richard	Lt RN	15.434	of the Amazon
Shannon A		26.515	
Shapter George		27.506	

Shaw John	Lt RN	14.86	
Shaw James		16.79	
Shaw	Capt	25.263	of the Auckland, packet
Shaw Anthony		26.515	
Shaw Isaac	Lt RN	30.80	
		30.88	
Shawe Matthew		13.410	
Shea John Linyee	Lt	5.439	
Sheakland		34.352	of Ringston, Canada
Shearer Robert		29.258	
Sheckley John		28.359	of the US Frigate Chesapeake
Shefton Thomas		29.258	
Sheills Ludlow	Lt RN	37.339	
Shelley	Mr	10.175	father-in-law to Mr Garthshore, one of the Lords of the Adm'y
Sheppard M A		11.494	
Sheriff	Capt RN	19.176	of the Curieux
Sheriff	Mrs	28.352	widow of Gen Sheriff
Sheriff George		34.352	of the HEIC
Shermer	Lt	2.448	
Sherry Thomas		27.506	
Sherwin Peter		26.351	
Shields John		29.352	
Shingles William		29.78	
Shipley Conway	Capt	19.440	
Shippard Alex G R		25.87	
Shippard Thomas		26.83	
Shirley H R		20.167	
Shooley William		31.425	
Shore Francis		26.433	
Short	Mrs	18.268	wife of Capt J Short
Shortland (senior)	Capt RN	9.165	
Shortland John	Capt	23.264	
Shortland	Lt RN	36.518	of the Tigris
Shortman William		15.257	
Shoveller	Mrs	25.440	wife of William Shoveller
Shoveller	Mrs	29.176	an old inhabitant of Portsea
Shove E	Mr	11.494	
Shrowder William		28.434	
Shuldham	Adm Lord	1.88	
		1.176	
Shuldham W		12.87	
		12.142	
Shute Fowler		27.438	
Sibley	Mrs	35.176	aged 80 years. Daughter of Admiral Reynolds
Sibrell	Lt	25.515	of the Piercer
Simens Thomas	Lt	14.429	
		14.438	
Simmens John		14.437	
Simmonds Thomas		7.85	
Simmonds	Mr	13.166	a Quartermaster, Portsmouth Dock Yard
Simmonds John	Mr	21.520	
Simmonds R	Lt	31.352	

Simms Samuel		6.260	
Simpson	Mrs	1.348	wife of Capt John Simpson RM
Simpson T		15.440	infant son of
Simpson G	Lt	20.80	
Simpson Robert	Capt RN	23.440	
Simpson	Mr	28.440	of the Bucephalus
Simpson John	Landman	31.426	on the Hannibal
Simpson John		32.512	at Stonehouse. He accompanied Commodore Byron on the Dolphin, 1766
Sims	Lt RN	16.88	p.o.w. at Verdun
Sinclair	Lt RM	6.62	of the Beaulieu
Sinclair D	Ensign	22.169	of the 71st Foot
Sison Edward		38.511	
Skelton Wm	Lt RN	20.494	
		21.87	
Skene John	Lt	24.352	of the 42nd Highland Regmt
Skinner	Mr	21.264	Royal Marine surgeon
Skinner F O G	Capt RN	23.520	
Skinner John		26.77	
Skinner Edward		29.78	
Skottowe George	Lt RN	38.348	
Skrymsher	Lt	15.87	
Skynner Lancelot	Capt	2.548	
Slack Mathew		26.440	
Slade J		17.264	
Slade	Miss	27.176	eldest daughter of Capt of the Experiment
Slanwood William		12.317	
Slater Magnus		21.343	
Slater William		29.82	
Slyde James		15.434	
Smart	Mr	19.264	of the Diamond
Smith	Lt	5.187	at Greenwich Hospital
Smith W	Capt	5.280	
Smith J		7.452	son of Capt J Smith of the victualling service between Cork and Plymouth
Smith R	Mid	10.517	of the Centaur
Smith	Lt	12.87	First of the Centaur
Smith	Lt RN	12.142	of the Centaur
Smith John	Private	13.410	RM on the Cleopatra
Smith James		14.258	
Smith Robert		14.437	
Smith	Lt	15.87	of the Namur
Smith Thomas		15.257	seaman of the Northumberland
Smith J	Lt	16.514	
Smith	Mr	19.87	Sgn of the Anson
Smith J	Capt RN	19.440	
Smith Thomas		20.418	Landman of the Amethyst
Smith Edward	General	21.88	of 43rd Regmt of Foot
Smith Francis	Capt RN	23.88	
Smith John	Pte	24.346	HEIC artillery
Smith Daniel		24.515	
Smith Lewis S		25.264	

Smith Aaron		25.433	
Smith Richard	R Adm	26.88	
Smith William	Mid	26.261	of the Hotspur
Smith William		26.433	carpenter's mate of Galatea
Smith Thomas	Landman	26.433	on the Phoebe
Smith Charles	Lt RM	27.87	
Smith Matthew	Major	27.176	
Smith William		27.345	of the Active
Smith	Mrs	27.440	wife of Lt Smith RN
Smith	Mr	28.263	clerk of the Survey, Portsmouth
Smith John		28.348	of the Guerriere
Smith John		29.78	of the Macedonian
Smith Thomas		29.258	
Smith	Mrs	29.440	wife of W R Smith
Smith William		30.507	
Smith Joseph		31.88	
Smith W	Capt RN	31.352	
Smith J	Sgt RM	33.262	of the Endymion
Smith John		33.340	of the Norge
Smith W B	Doctor	35.352	
Smith W		36.174	of the Antelope
Smith Robert		37.86	
Smith Elizabeth	Mrs	37.87	widow of William Smith
Smylie	Lt RN	14.350	of the Cyaene
Smyth John Bever		24.352	
Snell Hewit		28.162	
Snell Francis J	Capt RN	39.264	
Sneyd William		29.258	
Snipe John	Doctor	14.174	
Snow	Miss	11.344	daughter of Lt Snow
Somerset John S	Capt RN	14.262	
Sommerville George	Lt RN	35.88	
Sommerville Philip	Capt	37.176	
Sotheby Thomas	Mrs	7.364	
Sotheron Caroline M	Mrs	27.515	
South Henry		26.258	
Southcote	Lt RN	39.498	at Teignmouth
Southee William	Mr	1.88	
		1.175	
Speare Richard		35.175	
Spearing George A	Lt	20.167	
Spearman J R		25.432	
Speek	Mrs	31.352	wife of Lt Speek RN
Spence Thomas	Capt RN	20.336	
Spence	Lt	22.520	of the St Juan
Spencer Benjamin	Lt RM	5.356	
Spencer R		6.147	
Spencer Richard		18.348	
Spillar William		25.341	
Spottiswoode Robert		14.350	
Sprecker	Lt	22.169	2nd Lt Bn, King's German Legion
Sprent George	Lt RN	37.264	
Sprott	Lt RN	25.264	of the Star
Spry	Lt Gen RM	26.433	
Spry Thomas	Capt RN	34.512	
Spurking Jeremiah		31.257	

Squarey William	Mr	25.264	
Squire Matthew	R Adm	3.240	
Squire R J	Lt RM	5.188	
Squires Charles		29.258	
Stackpole Hassard	Capt RN	31.512	
Stackpole Massey		31.512	
Stackpole	Lt RN	35.86	at Jamaica
Stackpoole Marianna	Miss	23.440	
Stackpoole Wm		37.440	
Stagg William	Lt RN	33.176	
Stammets Robert		27.506	
Standidge Samuel	Sir	5.187	
Stanhope John	R Adm	4.527	
Stanhope	Lady	23.176	mother of V Adm Sir HE S.
Stanhope	Miss	28.263	eldest daughter of Admiral Sir Henry Stanhope
Stanhope Henry E	V Adm Sir	33.88	
Stanning Anthony		23.170	
Stark George		20.494	
Starmen John		22.251	
Start Thomas		17.343	alias Joseph Dickens
Stedman Charles	Doctor RN	6.348	
Stedman G W	Lt	11.494	
Steer William		38.511	
Stephen John		32.511	
Stephens Anne	Mrs	3.80	
Stephens	Mr	12.166	Purser of the Carysfort
Stephens F	Mr	13.166	
Stephens Francis		18.520	late commiss. for victualling
Stephens F		19.87	
Stephens Philip	Sir	22.440	
Stephenson Thomas	Capt RN	21.176	
Stevens	Capt RN	9.81	of the Chichester
Stevens		9.81	son of Capt of the Chichester
Stevens Richard		20.80	
Steward	Mr	6.147	Mid on the Pompee
Stewart A J	Lt RN	4.528	son of the Earl of Londonderry
Stewart Robert		5.356	Master of the Ganges
Stewart John	Capt	26.351	
Stewart	Mrs	28.176	wife of Capt Wm Stewart
Stewart James	Lt RN	30.176	
Stewart William	Capt Lord	32.264	of the Conquestadore
Stewart William	Capt RN	32.264	of the San Josef
Stewart George	Lt RN	33.352	
Stewart C H		35.87	of the HEIC
Sticton	Mr	25.88	sailmaker of Sheerness
Stiles	Capt	10.517	
Stiles Jane	Mrs	35.352	
Still James		33.352	
Stirling James	Mr	1.88	
Stirling	Capt	12.432	of the Serapis
Stirling	Lt RN	22.138/176	of the Prometheus
Stocker	Mrs	36.518	widow of Capt Stocker RN
Stockham John	Capt	31.175	
Stodart J	Mr	21.176	
Stokoe William	Capt	27.351	

Stoney	Mrs	9.339	widow of Capt Stoney RN
Stopford M F	Miss	35.176	
Storcks R H	Lt RN	36.518	
Storkhill Thomas		29.78	
Storvey John		29.78	
Stow Ather	Master	32.264	
Stowey M	Mrs	14.512	
Stratton Francis	Capt RN	5.464	
Strauchan	Capt	28.513	at Smyrna, ex p.o.w.
Stretch	Mrs	24.439	widow of Major Stretch
Strickland	Mrs	33.352	wife of T Strickland
Strong	Mr	11.87	Purser of the Galatea
Strong	Lt RM	13.504	of the Galatea
Strong John		26.261	
Strong	Mr	37.352	carpenter of the Q. Charlotte
Strutton William		14.167	
Stuart Nathaniel	Lt RN	1.175	
Stuart William	Lady	18.348	
Stuart Henry	Lord	22.176	
Stuart John	Capt RN	25.352	
Stuart C		27.515	
Stuart Charles	Capt	31.512	
Stubbs Samuel		14.258	
Stupart	Mrs	7.532	wife of Capt Stupart RN
Sulivan Daniel		19.342	
Sullings Edward		13.165	
Sullivan Matthew		16.439	
Sullivan John		28.82	
Sullivan	Mrs	36.264	mother of Capt TB S. RN
Summons Henry		24.440	
Sutherland James B	Mr	1.174	
Sutherland H E	Lt	16.88	
Sutton Edward		26.80	
Swaffield J		17.176	
Swanton	Colonel	5.188	of the Guards
Sweedland Henry J	Lt RN	31.88	
Sweet	Capt RM	28.352	of the Fame
Sweet	Capt RM	29.176	see also 28.352
Swiney	Lt	14.174	of the Prevost
Syme	Lt RM	4.256	
Symes Benjamin	Lt	11.494	
Symes Joseph	Capt RN	29.512	
Symons Henry		33.340	
Symons John	V Adm	2.644	
Syms William		27.511	
Tahourdin William	Capt	11.494	
Tait Dalhousie	Lt	22.505	
		22.520	
Tait John		27.506	
Tait James		30.264	
Taitt James		30.176	
Talbot R	Mr	18.268	
Talbot Mary Ann		19.352	pensioner, served five years in the navy as a sailor
Talbot	Capt	22.169	of the 5th Foot

Talbot	Mr	30.522	of the Thais
Talbot J H	Lt RN	38.88	
Tancred Charles	Lt	3.420	
Tanner Nathaniel		19.263	of the HEIC
Tappen Samuel	Lt	25.264	
Tapscott John		22.137	
Taylor Mary	Mrs	1.175	
Taylor Edward		7.85	
Taylor James		14.258	
Taylor G	Mr	14.512	
Taylor Joseph		15.342	
Taylor Colin		20.418	
Taylor Archibald		24.164	
Taylor Henry		27.506	
Taylor Jacob		27.506	
Taylor George		29.348	
Taylor	Mrs	30.264	wife of Capt Taylor of the George, transport
Taylor Bridges W	Capt	31.352	
Taylor	Miss	37.518	daughter of Capt Taylor RN
Tebball Abraham		29.258	
Temple	Capt RN	21.87	of the Cresecnt
		22.88	
Temple J		29.176	
Templer	Capt	13.423	of the Gaelan
Templeton Robert		27.506	
Terrent William		12.413	
Terris	Capt	24.439	of the Stork
Terry William		26.433	
Terry George		31.349	
Terryl John		19.342	
Thelluson	Hon Mr	39.264	of the HMS Tiber
Therre Saul		29.258	
Thesiger Frederick	Capt RN	14.262	
Thomas Benjamin		14.258	
Thomas William		22.137	landman on the Bellerophon
Thomas John	Adm	24.352	
Thomas William		25.434	landman on the Volage
Thomas George	Lt	37.352	
Thompson C	V Adm Sir	1.347	
Thompson	Mrs	2.448	wife of Capt Thompson RN
Thompson George		6.260	
Thompson J	Commander	11.494	
Thompson E	Mrs	14.511	wife of R Adm Thompson
Thompson John		16.79	
Thompson	Capt	18.437	
Thompson George	Reverend	20.336	
Thompson Henry		21.520	at Richmond, aged 14
Thompson John	Lt RN	22.88	
Thompson Henry		22.264	Purser of the Satellite
Thompson	Mr	24.352	Master of the Bucephalus
Thompson	Mr	26.439	Captain of the convict ship Captivity
Thompson Samuel	R Adm	30.176	
Thompson F	Lt RN	30.352	
Thompson Jane	Miss	33.352	

Name	Rank	Ref	Note
Thompson John	Lt RN	38.176	
Thong Thomas		20.167	
Thornborough	Lt RN	5.96	son of Adm Thornborough
Thornborough	Mrs	6.516	wife of R Adm T.
Thornborough	Mrs	30.522	wife of V Adm T.
Thornbury Charles		29.264	
Thornhill Cudbert		24.86	
Thornton James		14.262	
Thresher Maryanne	Miss	32.176	
Thurnham	Lt RM	13.166	
Tidy Thomas Holmes	Capt	18.174	
Tierney Peter		27.506	
Tillard	Capt	31.87	form. commander of the St Juan
Timins	Mrs	17.440	wife of Major Timins RM
Timpson	Mrs	36.87	wife of Col Timpson RM
Tipper John		12.87	
Tobin James		27.506	
Toby James		30.170	
Todd	Mr	24.175	Sgn of the Alfred
Toll Ashburnham N		3.80	
Tomlin Olivia	Mrs	6.260	
Tomlinson Philip		18.252	
Tomlinson R	Capt RN	30.522	
Tomykins Bohemyn	Mr	19.515	
Tonken Ann	Mrs	8.440	
Tonken John		25.88	
Tonyn Patrick	Capt	23.264	
Toole Thomas		15.434	
Toole David		26.174	
Tooley Richard	Lt RN	20.424	
Torbuct William		17.336	
Torrington John	Viscount	29.88	
Tosh Alexander		15.257	
Totty	R Adm	8.88	
Touche de la	Lt	11.494	
Touzeau Charles	Lt RN	33.88	
Towle E	Lt	28.513	
Townsend William		17.336	
Townshend Charles F		37.352	
Townson William		20.419	
Towry George Henry		21.352	
Towry G P		37.264	aged 84 years
Tracey John Smith		25.263	
Tracey Thomas		25.434	
Trafalgar	Lord Vis	19.87	
Trant Philip Henry		4.256	RM
Treby Trelawney		6.260	
Tregent Richard J	Lt	29.88	
Tregent H J	Lt RM	39.498	
Tremlett	Mr	24.516	Superintending Master, Plymouth
Tremlett	Lt RN	36.86	at Exeter
Trepass George		13.410	
Trevathick William	Lt RN	37.87	
Trevick William		30.170	

Name	Rank	Ref	Notes
Treville La Touche	Adm	12.255	of the French Navy
		12.299	
Trewren William	Lt RN	29.88	
Trickey B	Mr	24.88	
Triko Lewis		31.83	
Trippurst Edward		15.258	
Trotten	Miss	14.512	daughter of Capt Trotten RN
Trotter Alexander	Lt Col RM	7.364	
Trotter	Mrs	12.342	widow of Capt T. RN
Trotter	Major	18.240	of the 37th Light Bn
Troughton Thomas		16.515	last survivor of the Inspector, privateer, said to be 141 yrs old
Troughton T		20.424	at Plymouth
Truscott William	Lt RN	26.351	
Truscott Charles	Doctor	28.263	
Tryon Robert	Lt	25.175	
Tuck	Lt RM	5.188	
Tuck Joseph		28.348	
Tucker	Mrs	22.352	wife of Benjamin Tucker
Tucker John		25.515	
Tucker Mary	Mrs	33.440	widow of Capt Tudor Tucker
Tucker	Mr	38.88	aged 91, father of Benjamin Tucker
Tuckett George	the Hon	5.356	
Tuckey H	Capt RN	37.86	
Tully William		16.169	
Tupper	Lt RN	39.494	of the Victory
Turnbull Henry		2.172	RN
Turner John	Lt	6.435	
Turner Charles	Lt RN	20.80	
Turner Peter		22.138	
Turner Thomas		27.345	
Turner E	Lt RN	34.352	
Turner Joseph	Capt RN	35.440	
Turner	Lady	38.348	widow of Sir B Turner
Turnor John	Lt RN	6.435	
Turnour Henry	Lt RN, Hon	14.262	
Twigg Robert		29.502	
Twysden	Capt RN	6.348	
Tyson John		32.440	
Tyson	Mrs	36.87	widow of John Tyson
Ugler George		15.257	
Uniacke Robert		33.340	
Unthank Richard		25.432	
Upham William		15.258	
Urquhart	Lt RM	13.85	
Urquhart John		24.352	
Urry John	Capt RN	5.187	retired
Usher H T		6.348	
Uvedale	R Adm	20.494	
		21.87	
Uzuld Uzariah	Capt RN	1.446	
Vaillant Isaac	R Adm	12.511	

Valentee		26.433	
Valentine	Mrs	12.166	wife of John Valentine, Store keeper of the Victualling Office at Portsmouth
Valentine T		31.352	
Vandeput George	Adm	3.331	
		3.516	
Van Fleylen Henry		15.434	
Varley	Mr	9.81	Sgn's mate of the Chichester
Varley James		26.433	
Vaughan Johanna	Mrs	2.548	
Vaughan	Mr	8.439	Sgn at Gibraltar
Vaughan	Mrs	8.439	widow of above
Vaughan W M		24.175	
Vaughan J T		31.257	
Vautier Daniel		29.264	
Veitch Hall		29.352	
Venables Thomas		25.264	
Verniondes Wistre		25.434	
Vernour	Capt	10.175	
Veryfer Thomas		22.137	
Vezey Matthew		22.250	
Victor	Lt RN	33.352	of the Majestic
Vidal Emerie		26.88	
Vignoles	Lt RN	33.512	of the Bombay
Vinburgh Andrew		15.258	
Vincent George		17.347	
Vincent Nicholas	Adm	21.352	
Vinicombe	Mrs	31.512	mother of Lt Col V. RM
Virtue Benjamin	Lt	27.176	
Vivian Roger		29.257	
Vyvian	Lt RM	5.253	of the Melpomene
Waddell William		35.516	
Waddy	Mr	12.511	
Waghorn	Miss	1.176	dau of Capt Martin W.
Wainwright John	Capt RN	24.88	
Wainwright Mary	Mrs	38.88	
Wakely Jeremiah		15.258	
Waldegrave	Lt Hon	21.176	
Waldron William		25.434	
Waldron Joseph	Lt RN	40.243	
Wales John	Capt	24.87	of the HEIC
Walker	Doctor	3.240	
Walker Richard		17.343	
Walker Harry	Lt	17.347	
Walker John		24.87	of the HEIC
Walker James		26.258	
Walker Matilda	Miss	29.352	
Walker Robert		38.348	
Wall Andrew		2.439	
Wallace James	Adm Sir	9.251	
Wallace Thomas		12.255	
Wallace Robert		12.255	
Wallace James		30.85	
Waller	Capt	1.88	of HMS Saturn

Waller	Mr	20.168	retired Purser
Wallington Richard		25.432	
Wallis M	Mrs	13.166	widow of P Wallis Master Ship-wright, Halifax, N.S.
Wallis	Lt	18.174	of the Britannia
Wallis John		29.78	
Walpole	Capt RN, Hon	32.176	
Walsh John (senior)	Capt	1.176	
Walter John		25.263	
Walter	Mrs	28.263	widow of Capt Walter
Warburton Robert	Capt RN	18.520	
Warcup George	Lt RN	27.88	
Ward James		7.78	
Ward Salathiel	Mr	18.437	Asst Surgeon
Ward Charles	Master	19.87	
Ward Richard		20.419	
Ward John		28.82	
Wardell J W		30.264	
Warden William		18.519	
Warren	Mr	6.62	Mid on the Robust
Warren Diana	Miss	7.532	
Warren James		29.78	
Warren Samuel		29.348	
Waterhouse	Capt RN	28.264	
Waters John		15.257	
Waterson Thomas		33.340	
Watherstone Thos		32.511	
Watkins Thomas		16.79	
Watson Edward	Mr	1.175	
Watson H		4.168	
Watson	Mr	12.432	Master of the Pegase, Prison Ship, Portsmouth
Watson J B	Lt RM	20.256	
Watson	Capt RM	23.88	of the Polyphemus
Watson W B		27.88	
Watson George		29.78	
Watson Henry		35.264	
Watson W	Mr	39.343	
Watson Joshua R	Capt	39.498	
Watt William		13.165	
Watt G T L	Lt	30.84	
Watt S E	Capt RN	30.264	
Watts John	Lt RN	2.82	
Watts	Capt RN	5.544	one of Capt James Cook's officers
Watts Robert		22.251	
Watts Walter	Capt RN	31.512	
Watts	Capt	32.352	of the Jaseur
Waugh	Mr	12.342	shipwright of Portsea
Way William	Lt RN	32.440	
Webber William		24.176	
Webster Gilbert		12.87	
Webster James		17.343	
Webster William		40.74	
Weir Henry	Capt RM	8.176	
Weir James		26.433	

Welch	Robert	Mr	21.520	
Welch		Capt	23.176	of the Racoon
Welch	John		29.257	
Welladvice	J		19.87	
Wells	Thomas John		23.520	
Wells	Thomas	V Adm	26.433	
Wells	John		29.78	
Wells	David		29.258	
Wells	St Vincent		31.439	
			32.176	
Wells	James		36.86	
Wemys	C	Capt RN	7.532	
Wemyss		Mrs	10.87	wife of Gen Wemyss RM
Wemyss	Francis	Capt RN	37.176	
West	Henry	Capt RN	9.166	
Westbeach	Joseph	Capt RN	26.515	
Westcott		Mrs	29.352	mother of Capt Westcott, who fell at the Nile
Western	Thomas	R Adm	33.88	
Weston	William		29.348	
Westonberg		Mr	29.264	dispenser of Bermuda Hosp
Wetheral	Frederick		19.259	
Wetherall		Mr	22.440	Sgn of the Vestal
Wharton	Richard		26.433	
Wharton	Thomas		29.82	
Wheatley	William		24.516	
Wheteridge	Thomas		17.347	
Whetter		Capt RN	5.544	
Whinyates	G B	Capt RN	20.167	
Whipple	Thomas		14.437	
Whitaker	Thomas		27.507	
Whitby		Capt RN	15.352	
Whitby		Mrs	23.88	wife of Capt W. and second daughter of Commissioner Inglefield
Whitby	Henry	Capt	27.440	
White		Mr	12.511	
White	A S	Lt RN	20.253	
White		Mrs	21.176	wife of Capt White RN and fourth daughter of Commissioner Fanshaw
White	William	Lt RN	21.520	
White	John		22.137	
White	C	Capt RN	23.520	
White		Mrs	25.176	wife of Capt White RN
White	William		28.348	captain of the fore-castle of Guerriere
White	James		29.258	
White	John		30.448	
White	George		31.172	
White		Mr	32.512	aged 94 years. Father of Capt T White RN
White	William		37.88	of the HEIC
White		Mr	37.176	gunner of the Apollo
Whitehouse	Jeremiah		27.506	
Whiting	Joshua		38.348	

Whitshed James B H		31.176	
Whittman Josiah	Capt	23.440	
Wickham	Miss	39.176	niece of the late Lt W. RN
Wight	Mrs	27.515	wife of Capt Wight RN
Wilby John	Lt	12.432	
Wilcox James	Lt RN	27.88	
Wiley Thomas		31.511	
Wilkie Alexander		37.429	
		37.434	
Wilkins William	Lt RM	22.250	
		22.352	
Wilkins John	Lt RN	33.512	
Wilkins Richard F	Lt RM	38.511	
Wilkinson William	Capt RN	35.264	
Willes J		12.511	
		13.165	
Willes Thomas	Mr	22.88	
Willes Cornelius	Lt RN	24.88	
Williams J D	Lt RM	6.147	
Williams	Mr	6.172	Mid on the Medusa
Williams John		6.239	Master of the Intrepid
Williams S		13.246	
Williams	Lt	14.174	Agent for Transports, Barbadoes
Williams Woodford	Lt	18.174	of the Spartan
Williams William		19.342	
Williams	Lt RN	19.342	
Williams Ann	Miss	20.494	
Williams Walker		22.138	
Williams William		22.251	
Williams John		24.168	marine on the Montagu
Williams Charles	Lt RN	24.176	
Williams Poulton	Lt RN	24.439	
Williams Evan		25.434	
Williams M A	Mrs	26.179	
Williams John		26.433	seaman on the Astraea
Williams Peter		27.345	
Williams Hugh		29.258	
Williams Edward		30.81	
Williams	Mr	30.264	former Master of the Lord Hobart
Williams	Mrs	31.352	mother of Lt Col Richard Williams RM
Williams Richard	Capt RN	32.512	
Williams	Lt RM	37.434	
Williamson James		14.429	
		14.438	
Williamson John		15.258	
Williamson	Capt	18.240	of the 36th Regmt
Williamson	Mrs	19.176	widow of Capt James W. HEIC
Williamson Thomas	Capt	27.440	
Willoughby Thomas		16.169	
Willoughby Ferris		33.352	
Wills M	Lt RN	8.352	
Wills	Lt RN	14.262	
Wills George	Lt RN	29.257	
		29.264	

Wilmot	Capt	2.439	of the Alliance
Wilmot Benjamin		36.518	
Wilmot Alexander A		39.423	
Wilmott David	Capt RN	2.172	
Wilson	Mr	10.175	
Wilson Charles	Lt	11.494	
Wilson S		12.342	
Wilson James		12.413	
Wilson	Mr	12.511	
Wilson John		16.349	
Wilson M		17.347	
Wilson Robert		20.168	
Wilson Henry	Capt HEIC	23.440	
Wilson W	Mr	25.87	
Wilson George		26.83	
Wilson Thomas		28.162	
Wilson John		29.257	
Wilson	Capt RM	36.259	of the Leander
Wiltshire William	Lt RM	12.317	
Winchester Charles		3.80	
Windsor Thomas	Capt	21.88	of the 10th or Ryl Veteran Bn
Windsor Thomas	Capt	21.88	his eldest daughter
Wingrove George F	Lt Col RM	26.180	
Winkeworth James		24.255	
Winkworth	Capt	8.176	
Wintle E	Lt RN	39.264	
Winton Ebenezer L	Lt RN	39.423	
Wintour Charles F	Lt RN	38.176	
Wistinghausen A	Lt RN	17.520	
Withers	Lt	9.251	of the Emerald
Witherston Edward	Lt RN	32.440	
Witley Edward		13.410	
Wittman	Mrs	7.532	wife of Capt W. RN
Witton Charles		22.251	
Wolfe Jacob	Capt	1.348	
Wolseley Charles	Adm	19.352	
Wood John		2.448	
Wood John		12.317	Ord Seaman on the Maidstone
Wood Samuel	Mr	23.520	
Wood John		27.88	
Wood	Mrs	33.352	sister of Capt Sir James Athol Wood RN
Woodcock William		28.348	
Woodford	Lt RN	18.235	of the Cruiser
		18.252	
Woodin John	Lt RN	14.437	
Woodis	Mrs	27.175	mother of Admirals Sir Edward and Israel Pellew
Woods Charles	Lt RN	32.439	
Woodward Samuel		26.83	
Woodward George		29.348	
Woodward Thomas	Lt	32.340	of the 4th Regmt
Wooldridge F	Capt	13.246	
Woolridge James	Capt RN	32.352	
Wordsworth	Capt	13.335	of the Abergavenny
Worsley William M	Lt	24.264	

Worth Joseph		17.439	
Worth Thomas	Lt RM	25.87	
Wrangel	Adm	2.82	
Wray	Mrs	4.256	wife of Capt Wray
Wright P W	Lt RN	18.85	
Wright Charles		18.348	
Wright Hodgson		18.520	Surgeon
Wright	Mr	19.264	of the Diamond
Wright James		24.352	
Wright John		26.433	
Wright	Dr & Mrs	29.84	drowned near New Brunswick
Wright J C		32.176	
Wright John		33.172	
Wrottesley Edward	Capt	32.176	
		32.264	
Wyatt George		16.81	
Wye William B		28.352	
Wylde John	Mr	18.520	Assistant Surgeon
Wylliams Cooper	Reverend	36.174	
Wynter Delamore	Capt RN	23.440	
Wynward C		3.156	
Yates Vernon G	Lt RN	8.520	
Yates	Capt HEIC	25.176	
Yates L M	Lt RN	28.439	
Yates Lenox M B	Lt	30.172	
Yates Mary	Mrs	30.176	
Yaulden Henry		5.356	
Yeo William	Capt RN	19.515	Retired
Yeo	Mrs	25.264	Matron of the Naval Asylum
Yeo James L	Sir	40.243	
Yonge	Lt RN	19.264	of the Seahorse
Yorke Joseph S	Capt, MP	7.276	infant son of
Yorke	Mrs	27.176	wife of Adm Sir JS Yorke
Yorke Horatio N	Master	31.352	
Young George	Lt RN	1.176	
Young George	Capt RM	4.348	
Young	Mr	9.423	Sgn of the Bellerophon
Young	Lt RM	12.342	
Young	Mrs	13.246	wife of Col Young RM
Young Daniel		22.259	
Young William	Mr	23.88	
Young George	Adm Sir	24.88	
Young William	Sir	26.88	footnote **26.**180
Young George		27.506	
Young	Mr	28.176	Purser of the Rodney
Young John		30.85	
Young William		30.85	
Young	Mrs	32.440	widow of Adm James Young
Young Robert	Lt RN	33.440	
Young Charles	Lt RN	35.264	
Young Susannah	Mrs	37.352	
Young	Lt RN	38.348	at Poole
Younghusband	Capt RN	16.176	
Younghusband	Mrs	29.176	wife of Capt Younghusband RN
Yowel Gregory		19.259	

Appendices

Affleck Edmund	R Adm Sir	21.445
Affleck Philip	Adm	21.445
Allen John Carter	Adm	23.177
Alms James (senior)	Capt	2.549
Anson George	Adm Lord	8.266
Arbuthnot Marriot	Adm	23.265
Ashworth Henry	Lt	33.264
Balchen John	Adm Sir	28.89
Barrett John	Capt RN	37.177
Barrington Samuel	Adm	4.169
Bazely John	V Adm	14.177
Benbow John	V Adm	20.169
Berkeley George C	R Adm Hon	12.89
Berry Edward	Capt Sir	15.177
		15.352
Bertie Thomas	R Adm	26.1
Bettesworth	Capt RN	39.425
Bickerton Richard	R Adm Sir	13.337
Blake Robert	Adm	31.1
Bligh Richard Rodney	Adm	13.425
Blyth Samuel	Commander RN	32.441
Boscawen Edward	Adm Hon	7.181
Bouillon Philip D'Auvergne	Duke of	13.169
Bowen Richard	Capt	23.353
Boyle Courtenay	Capt RN,Hon	30.1
Boyles Charles	V Adm	38.265
Brisbane Charles	Capt Sir	20.81
Broke Philip Bowes	Capt RN Sir	33.1
Brodie David	Capt	3.81
Brooking Samuel	Capt RN	10.177
Buckoll Richard	Capt	2.85
Budge William		35.1
		35.89
Buller Edward	Capt RN	19.177
Bury Richard Incledon	R Adm	29.177
Byron George Anson	Capt	6.26
Calder Robert	V Adm Sir	17.89
		27.441
Caldwell Benjamin	Adm	11.1
Campbell Robert	Capt RN	36.441
Christian Hugh Cloberry	R Adm Sir	21.177
Cochrane	Capt RN, Hon Lord	22.1
Coffin Isaac	R Adm Sir	12.1
Collier George	V Adm Sir	32.265
		32.353
Collingwood Cuthbert	V Adm Lord	15.353
Colpoys John	Adm Sir	11.265
Cook James	Capt	9.1
Cooke John	Capt	17.353
Cornish Samuel Pitchford	Adm Sir	11.345
Cornwallis William	Adm Hon	7.1
Cosby Phillips	Adm	14.353
Cotton Charles	Adm Sir	27.353
Curtis Roger	V Adm Sir	6.261

Dacres James Richard	V Adm	26.265
Dacres Richard	Capt RN	26.353
		26.441
Dalrymple Alexander		35.177
Dalyell William Cavendish C	Capt RN	32.1
		32.89
Dance Nathaniel	Capt HEIC	12.345
Darby George	V Adm	23.89
Dartmouth George Legge	Lord	28.177
De Saumarez Philip	Capt RN	31.265
Digby Robert	Adm	11.89
Domett William	R Adm	15.1
Douglas Andrew	Capt Sir	25.353
Downman Hugh	Capt RN	21.1
Drake Francis	Sir	29.1
		29.265
		29.441
Duckworth John Thomas	V Adm Sir	18.1
Duff George	Capt	15.265
Duncan Adam	Lord Viscount	4.81
Edgecumbe George	Adm Hon	22.177
(Earl of Mount Edgecumbe)		
Elliot John	Adm	9.425
Ellison Joseph	Capt	19.1
Fairfax William George	R Adm Sir	5.465
Faulknor Robert	Capt	16.1
Flinders Matthew	Capt RN	32.177
Forbes John	Adm Hon	25.265
Forrest Arthur	Capt RN	25.441
Forrest Austen	Capt HEIC	29.89
Fothergill William	Capt RN	38.349
Fraser Alexander	R Adm	31.89
Frederick Thomas Lenox	R Adm	37.265
		37.353
Gardner	V Adm Lord	8.177
Gardner Alan Hyde	R Adm Hon	21.357
Geary Francis	Adm Sir	17.177
Gordon James Alexander	Capt RN	31.353
Gower Erasmus	Sir	4.257
		30.265
Graham Edward Lloyd	Capt RN	29.353
Graves Thomas	Adm Lord	5.377
Graves Thomas	R Adm Sir	8.353
Greenly Isaac Coffin	R Adm Sir	12.1
Grey Edward	Commander RN	26.181
Haddock Nicholas	Adm	27.89
Hamilton Edward	Sir	5.1
Hardinge George Nicholas	Capt	20.257
Hardy Charles	Adm Sir	19.89
Harness John	Doctor	35.265
Harvey John	Capt	3.241
Hawke Edward	Adm Lord	7.453
Hawkins John	Adm Sir	37.1

Henderson Robert	Capt RN	38.177
Holloway John	V Adm	19.353
Holmes Robert	R Adm Sir	40.85
Hood Alexander Arthur	Lord Bridport	1.265
Hood Samuel	Lord Viscount	2.1
Hood Alexander	Capt RN	6.173
Hood Samuel	Commodore Sir	17.1
Hope William Johnstone	Capt RN	18.269
Horsburgh James	(Hydrographer to HEIC)	28.441
Hotham William	Adm Lord	9.341
Howard Charles	Earl of Nottingham	18.89
Howe	Earl	1.1.
Hughes Edward	Adm Sir	9.85
Humphreys Salusbury Pryce	Capt RN	28.353
Hunter John	Capt RN	6.349
Hunter William	Lt RN	13.1
Inman Henry	Capt RN	25.1
James William	Commod HEIC, Sir	3.89
Jennings John	R Adm Sir	40.1
Jervis John	Earl of St Vincent	4.1
Jervis William Henry	Capt	20.1
Keith	Admiral Lord	10.1
Kempenfelt Richard	R Adm	7.365
Keppel Augustus	Admiral Lord Visc	7.277
King Richard	Adm Sir	12.433
King William Elletson	Lt RN	30.449
Kingsmill Robert	Adm Sir	5.189
Knight John	R Adm	11.425
Knowles Charles	Adm Sir	1.89
		2.265
Laforey John	Adm Sir	25.177
Layman William	Capt RN	37.441
		38.1
		38.89
		39.177
Leake John	Adm Sir	16.441
Locker William	Commodore	5.97
Louis Thomas	R Adm Sir	16.177
Lydiard Charles	Capt	19.441
Macbride John	Adm	19.265
Mackenzie Thomas	R Adm	33.353
Mackenzie Kenneth	Capt RN	38.437
Manderson James	Capt RN	30.89
Milne David	R Adm Sir	36.353
Mitchell Andrew	Adm Sir	16.89
Moore John	Adm Sir	3.421
Mulgrave	Lord	8.89
Munday George	Capt	39.1
Murray George	R Adm	18.177

Thesiger Frederick	Capt RN Sir	14.441
Thompson Edward	Capt RN	6.437
		7.93
Thompson Thomas Boulden	Sir	14.1
Tomlinson Nicholas	Capt RN	25.89
Trollope Henry	V Adm Sir	18.353
Tromp Marten H van	Adm	37.89
Troubridge Thomas	R Adm Sir	23.1
Truscott William	R Adm	30.177
Tuckey James Hingston	Capt RN	40.165
		40.245
Turnor John	Capt RN	24.441
Tyrrel Richard	R Adm	10.353
Vernon Edward	Adm	9.169
Vincent Richard Budd	Capt	13.222
		17.265
Wallis Samuel	Capt RN	33.89
Walpole Richard	Capt HEIC, Hon	14.89
Warren John Borlase	Sir	3.333
		26.89
Warren Peter	V Adm Sir	12.257
Whitby Henry	Capt RN	28.265
Whitshed James Hawkins	V Adm	22.353
Wishart James	Adm Sir	27.177
Wood James Athol	Capt RN Sir	24.177
Wright John Wesley	Capt	**34** .1/ 89/ 176/ 265/ 353/ 441
		35.441
		36.1/89/177/265
Yeo James Lucas	Capt RN Sir	24.265
Young George	Adm Sir	31.177

List of 96 inmates aged 80 years and over, circa 1807, whose personal details are recorded in Volume 9:

Anderson William	391		Hutchins John	390
Archer James	390		Jackson John	390
Beaves John	392		Jeffrey William	392
Biggs John	392		Keith John	391
Blackwell John	390		Kindred Thomas	392
Blank P	391		Knight Francis	389
Bradley John	389		Lansdown Thomas	390
Brown William	389		Lee William	392
Bulger Joseph	391		Linnel William	389
Caldwell Robert	389		Lloyd John	389
Carbery John	390		M'Neal Daniel	390
Caryess Emmanuel	391		M'Nichols Nathan	392
Chapman Nathaniel	390		M'Pearson John	390
Collins Edward	390		Maddox Richard	389
Cooper Alexander	391		Mager John	392
Cooper Thomas	389		Malcum Adam	390
Coughlan Daniel	390		Martin Robert	391
Coverdale John	389		Mathews Charles	391
Cummings John	389		Moore Jeffery	390
Dawson James	389		Moore John	390
Decamp John	389		Murrey Owen	392
Dempsy James	391		Oldston Richard	390
Diffiny George	390		Padgett Robert	392
Durdon William	392		Patch James	390
Eager Peter	390		Pike Henry	391
Ferguson Edward	389		Plant John	391
Forbes Alexander	389		Pottle Robert	389
Forbes George	390		Richards Henry	391
Fowler Thomas	392		Richardson Peter	389
Gammon William	392		Riley James	391
Garvis John	392		Rogers John	391
Godler James	391		Rowelington William	392
Griffiths Robert	392		Rutter Isaac	390
Griffiths Thomas	392		Shuter John	389
Grisley Thomas	392		Smith David	391
Gullam John	389		Skinner Edward	390
Hacken Thomas	391		Smith Edward	391
Haddon John	391		Smith Isaac	392
Hagard John	391		Smith William	392
Hannaway Robert	390		Taylor George	389
Harford John	392		Toms Robert	389
Hasser Stephen	391		Vaughan Thomas	390
Hill Henry	392		Web John	392
Hillhouse James	392		Welch John	389
Hopkins Francis	392		Wellers John	392
Hunter Tub	391		Weneman George	391
Hunter William	389		Wright William	390
Hussey Frederick	389		Writt John	389

Specialist Booksellers

For a guide to printed sources of naval history and biography see Family
Tree Magazine (141 Great Whyte, Ramsey, Huntingdon, Cambridge
PE17 1HP) for September 1988.

United Kingdom

ALBION SCOTT LTD 51 York Road, Brentford, Middlesex TW8 OQP

FISHER NAUTICAL Huntswood House, St Helena Lane, Streat, Hassocks,
Sussex BN6 8SD

FRANCIS EDWARDS 13 Great Newport Street, Charing Cross Road, London
WC2H 7JA *and* The Old Cinema, Castle Street, Hay-on-Wye, via Hereford
HR3 5DF

G L GREEN 104 Pitshanger Lane, Ealing, London W5 1QX

MAGGS BROS 50 Berkeley Square, London W1X 6EL

MAINMAST BOOKS Saxmundham, Suffolk IP17 1HZ

MARINE BOOKS "Nilcoptra", 3 Marine Road, Hoylake, Wirral, Cheshire
L47 2AS

MOTOR BOOKS 33 St Martin's Court, London WC2N 4AL

MICHAEL PRIOR 34 Fen End Lane, Spalding, Lincs PE12 6AD

R & S PYKE 2 Beaufort Villas, Claremont Road, Bath, Avon BA1 6LY

ANTHONY J SIMMONDS 23 Nelson Road, Greenwich, London SE10 9JB

Polar Specialists

BLUNTISHAM BOOKS Oak House, Bluntisham, Huntingdon PE17 3LS

EXPLORER BOOKS Fallow Chase, Durfold Wood, Plaistow, West Sussex
RH14 OPL

GRENVILLE STREET BOOKSHOP Edgeley, Stockport, Cheshire SK3 9ET

P J WALCOT 60 Sunnybank Road, Sutton Coldfield, West Midlands B73 5RJ

United States of America

ACADIA BOOK SERVICE PO Box 244, Castine, Maine 04421

ARMCHAIR SAILOR 69 Lee's Wharf, Newport, Rhode Island 02840

CARAVAN - MARITIME BOOKS 87-06 168th Place, Jamaica, New York 11432

E J LEFKOWICZ INC PO Box 630, Fairhaven, MA 02719

Publications

AMERICAN NEPTUNE published quarterly by the Peabody Museum of Salem, 161 Essex Street, East India Square, Salem MA 01970, USA

INTERNATIONAL JOURNAL OF NAUTICAL ARCHAEOLOGY published quarterly by the Nautical Archaeology Society, c/o Council for British Archaeology, 112 Kennington Road, London SE11 6RE

HAKLUYT SOCIETY publication annually, c/o The Map Library, The British Museum, Great Russel Street, London WC1B 3DG

MARINER'S MIRROR published quarterly by The Society for Nautical Research, c/o The National Maritime Museum, Greenwich, London SE10 9NF

NAVAL HISTORY MAGAZINE published quarterly by United States Naval Institute, Annapolis, Maryland, 21402, USA

NAVY RECORDS SOCIETY publication annually, Hon Secy. c/o The Public Record Office, Chancery Lane, London WC2A 1LR

NELSON DISPATCH journal of the Nelson Society published quarterly, B Burgess MBE, 43 King Street, Norwich NR1 1PJ

POLAR RECORD published quarterly by The Scott Polar Research Institute, Lensfield Road, Cambridge CB2 1ER

THE REVIEW the quarterly journal of the Naval Historical Collectors and Research Association. Hon Sec and Editor, John T Mock, 17 Woodhill Avenue, Portishead, Bristol BS20 9EX